CONTENTS

LIST OF ABBREVIATIONS   vi

INTRODUCTION   vii

CHAPTER ONE   Traditional and current recruitment methods

Past trends   1
Current trends   3
Employment laws   4
The development of Human Resource Management (HRM)   6

CHAPTER TWO   Major influences on the labour market in the 1990s

Demography   10
The economy   12
Global mobility   13
New technology   14
Rehabilitation technology   15
National Vocational Qualifications (NVQs)   16
Leisure   17
Quality standards   19
Training Enterprise Councils (TECs)   20

CHAPTER THREE   Planning a successful recruitment campaign

The nature of human resources   23
Skills analysis/audit   24
Methods of recruitment   25
Application forms   26
Personnel specification forms   29
Interviewing   30
Recruitment and selection campaign checklist   32
Further reading   33

CHAPTER FOUR   Equal opportunities issues

What are equal opportunities?   34
An equal opportunities policy   35
The law on equal opportunities   36
Sexual harassment   39
The Equal Pay Act 1970   39
Opportunity 241   40
The government commissions   41
Maternity rights   42
Parental leave   44
Other types of discrimination   45
European Community measures   51
Further reading   52

CHAPTER FIVE   The employment contract and terms and conditions of employment

What is a contract?	53
The employment contract	54
The Advisory, Conciliation and Arbitration Service (ACAS)	63
Dismissal	64
Redundancy	67
Further reading	68

CHAPTER SIX   Investing in training

The induction period	70
Staff appraisal	72
Positive action	76
Internal and external training resources	79
Training Needs Audit (TNA)	82
Investors in People	83
Sources of training	83
Further reading	85

CHAPTER SEVEN   Personnel records and data protection

Personnel records	86
Data protection	89

CHAPTER EIGHT   Grievance and disciplinary procedures

Formal agreement procedures	96
Grievance procedures	98
Disciplinary procedures	100
Trade unions	102
Industrial tribunals	105

CHAPTER NINE   Effective people management

Job satisfaction	108
Methods of improving morale	112
Putting policy into practice	115

CHAPTER TEN   Welfare at work

Welfare provision	119
Trade union activity	123
Employers' associations	124
Health and Safety legislation	125
European Community law	129
Other welfare issues	130
Further reading	131

CHAPTER ELEVEN   Rewards for work

Pay	132
Holidays	139
Further reading	139

CHAPTER TWELVE   External influences on the UK labour market

The single European market   141
World economic developments   145
Further reading   148

CHAPTER THIRTEEN   Recommendations for effective HRM

Summary   149
Further reading   152

APPENDICES

Appendix 1   Glossary of terms   153
Appendix 2   Acts of Parliament   156
Appendix 3   Useful addresses   157

LIST OF ABBREVIATIONS

ACAS	Advisory, Conciliation and Arbitration Service
BGP	Business Growth Programme
BTEC	Business and Technology Education Council
BITC	Business In The Community
CAADE	Campaign Against Age Discrimination in Employment
CBI	Confederation of British Industry
COSHH	Control Of Substances Hazardous to Health
CRE	Commission for Racial Equality
CSE	Certificate of Secondary Education
DAS	Disablement Advisory Service
DPA	Disabled Persons Act
DRO	Disablement Resettlement Officer
EAT	Employment Appeal Tribunal
EC	European Commission
ECU	European Currency Unit
EEF	Engineering Employers Federation
EIC	European Information Centre
EOC	Equal Opportunities Commission
EPA	Equal Pay Act
EWC	Expected Week of Confinement
GCSE	General Certificate of Secondary Education
GNVQ	General National Vocational Qualification
GOQ	Genuine Occupational Qualification
HASAWA	Health And Safety At Work Act
HELIOS	Handicapped People Living Independently in an Open Society
HIV	Human Immunodeficiency Virus
HMSO	Her Majesty's Stationery Office
HRM	Human Resource Management
HSE	Health and Safety Executive
IT	Industrial Tribunal
JES	Job Evaluation Study
LECs	Local Employment Companies
NACRO	National Association for the Care and Resettlement of Offenders
NALGO	National Association of Local Government Officers
NCVQ	National Council of Vocational Qualifications
NOW	New Opportunities for Women
NVQ	National Vocational Qualification
PACT	Placing, Assessment and Counselling Team
PRA	Pre-Retirement Association
QW	Qualifying Week
RDP	Register of Disabled Persons
RIDDOR	Reporting of Injuries, Diseases and Dangerous Occurences Regulations
RRA	Race Relations Act
RSI	Repetitive Strain Injury
SCOTVEC	Scottish Vocational Education Council
SDA	Sex Discrimination Act
SMP	Statutory Maternity Pay
SVQ	Scottish Vocational Qualification
TECs	Training and Enterprise Councils
TNA	Training Needs Audit
TUC	Trades Union Congress
TVEI	Technical Vocational Educational Initiative
VAT	Value Added Tax
WAMT	Women And Manual Trades
WIM	Women Into Management
WISE	Women Into Science and Engineering

INTRODUCTION

Nowadays, it is widely acknowledged that staff are an organisation's most important resource and most valuable asset. Human resource managers (amongst others) recognise that investment in staff is just as important as investment in plant and machinery. Effective human resource management is about enabling each and every member of staff to reach his or her potential and make a key contribution towards company survival and growth in an increasingly competitive world.

In the current ever changing economic climate, human resource management is rather similar to crisis management. That is, it is an attempt to bring back, as best one can, order, logic and direction to a situation where population changes, declining birth rates, a reduction in school leavers, skill shortages, increasing world competition and the single European market, to mention just a few of the factors, are changing the entire structure of employment and the labour market. These issues have an immediate impact upon all organisations, whatever their size or the nature of their business. In turn, they call for suitable human resource strategies to be established in order that companies can ensure that their future needs can be met by their staff.

This book will guide any student involved in human resource issues through the challenges created by changes in the labour market. It attempts to assist the new human resource manager to develop his or her confidence and competence in managing, motivating and directing people. It examines the many changes affecting the world of work and suggests ways of coping with change through employee participation in company plans and decision making.

Human Resource Management discusses employment law and the legislation on equality of opportunity at work, health and safety and data protection. Discussion points and exercises are included throughout the book to stimulate further debate and investigation into current employment practices.

TRADITIONAL AND CURRENT RECRUITMENT METHODS

PAST TRENDS

If we were to look at the history of work over the past century we would notice a number of patterns emerging. Events on a worldwide scale have influenced the labour market, and wars have been a major factor.

Some of the events of the past one hundred years include:

1903	Women's Social and Political Union was formed in Britain by the suffragette leader, Emmeline Pankhurst
1906	First Labour Members of Parliament were elected in British general election; Labour Party formed
1909	Old age pensions were introduced in Britain
1914–1918	World War One
1919	League of Nations founded
1921	Irish free state established
1924	First Labour government in Britain
1926	General Strike in Britain
1939–1945	World War Two
1945	The United Nations Organisation was formed in an attempt to maintain peace throughout the world and foster cooperation between different nations. Its Charter was signed by 50 nations
1957	Treaty of Rome signed by Belgium, France, West Germany, Italy, Luxembourg and Netherlands established the European Economic Community (the Common Market)
1973	Britain, Ireland and Denmark joined EEC
1987	The Single European Act is established
1989	The reunification of East and West Germany
1990	The Gulf War
1992	The single European market is formed

These are just a few of the events which have shaped our history in the last hundred years. Each of these events, in their own particular way, has influenced the world of work either directly or indirectly. The type of work which is pursued nowadays is very different from that which was undertaken even 50 years ago. Heavy manufacturing, mining and agriculture were the dominant industries in which many people worked after the Industrial Revolution and even until after the Second World War. Before the middle of the last century children also worked in factories and it wasn't until the Factories Act of 1833 that children under the age of nine were forbidden to be employed in factories.

As well as world events, local conditions also influence the type of work which people do. In the UK for example, industries such as mining, fishing, shipbuilding and agriculture are determined by the geography of an area. Mining areas dominate much of Yorkshire and South Wales, and shipbuilding is concentrated in coastal areas. In the past, these local concentrations of work have provided employment for generations of families. However, the danger of relying on a single industry rather than a variety of industries has become apparent when an industry has experienced problems. In this event, entire communities can suddenly find themselves out of work, with little prospect of alternative employment locally.

EXERCISE

What are the traditional industries in your area? If possible, find out how many people are employed in them. Also, try and find out how many people were employed in them fifty or so years ago. This information may be available in the local library. Present your findings in report form to your group.

In the past, the job which a person did was generally determined by what his or her family did. Traditionally, boys did the same type of work as their fathers, and more often than not, as their grandfathers as well. It was also common practice to stay in the same job for the whole of one's working life. For employers and factory owners this made life easy insofar as recruitment and selection were concerned, since they were guaranteed a constant supply of labour.

In the majority of cases, women did not work outside the home, except as governesses or nannies. This all changed during the wars when men were on active service, and women took over the running of factories and made up a large proportion of the labour force. There was also a rapid development in women's employment in the post-war years. At first, the bulk of jobs were filled by single women but throughout the 1950s and 1960s the number of married women in paid work increased steadily. However, the jobs available to them were mainly those which were considered 'women's work', such as in the service industries, light industry and in offices, and as the welfare state was developed, in teaching, social services and healthcare.

In some parts of the world, women's contribution to the war effort was acknowledged, and many women maintained a high profile in employment even after the war had ended. In many countries however, women were forced to return to the unpaid world of housework as soon as men returned from war to reclaim their jobs in industry. Since the end of the Second World War, an increasing number of women work outside the home in either part-time or full-time paid employment.

Do some background research then give your group a five minute talk on one of the following subjects:

- How the nature of work has changed in the last 20 years.
- What is meant by men's work and women's work?
- 'In a few years time, the new technology available will enable everyone to work at home via a computer network.' What are the advantages and disadvantages of this situation should it become true?

CURRENT TRENDS

The world of employment and the labour market have both changed dramatically in the last 50 years. Occupations which have traditionally been heavily male dominated, such as engineering and construction, now have growing numbers of women entering them. Similarly, in the higher paid jobs, many women are now reaching the same positions as men and demanding high status jobs too.

From once having a manufacturing industrial base, Britain is now increasingly becoming service industry based. As a result, more people now work in the service sectors such as banking and insurance, than in heavy manufacturing industries like steel and mining.

Write a list of as many 'new' jobs you can think of which were unheard of 50 years ago. What factors have influenced the growth of new jobs?

Inventions and discoveries both create new jobs and make other ones disappear. Look at some of the inventions since 1900:

1901	Vacuum cleaner
1903	Aeroplane
1908	Cellophane
1911	Combine harvester
1913	Geiger counter
1925	Television
1925	Frozen food process
1935	Nylon
1944	Automatic digital computer
1946	Electronic computer
1947	Polaroid camera
1948	Transistor

1955   Hovercraft
1955   Contraceptive pill
1956   Videotape recording

Even before these inventions, many other items were already coming onto the market: the safety match, sewing machines, washing machines, typewriters, margarine, telephones, cash registers, fountain pens, motorcycles and pneumatic tyres, to name just a few. In time, each of them created new jobs, in design, manufacture, sales, and more recently, in quality control. Each product is continually being improved as researchers, designers and quality controllers strive to enhance their products and keep them up to date.

EXERCISE

Try and find pictures in old history and geography books of some of the first products named above. Notice how different they look to today's models. In general, each new version of an invention tends to be smaller and more compact than the original model. For example, the first electronic computers, invented in 1946, were taller than an average man; compare this to the laptop computers which are available today. Collect pictures and photographs of as many products you can find. Draw up a checklist called 'compare and contrast', and list the similarities and differences between today's models and those invented 20 or 30 years ago.

Each new invention has influenced the office environment as well as the shop floor. Nowadays, almost without exception, all offices are equipped with a whole range of devices such as telephones, fax machines, photocopiers, telex machines, word processors, printers, and other devices unheard of in the past. Many new inventions such as washing machines, dishwashers and microwave ovens have been called labour-saving devices. Many of the latest devices originated in Japan, Germany, the USA and the UK. In the past, much housework was done by hand and was extremely time consuming: a whole day taken for clothes washing alone was standard.

DISCUSSION POINT

What has been the impact of labour-saving devices on housework? What affects have they had on the labour force?

EMPLOYMENT LAWS

As new inventions are continually being discovered, new laws have been introduced to impose rules and regulations on users to handle them correctly and safely. Today there are dozens of laws which relate to a whole range of employment practices: health and safety, hours of work, pensions, data protection, equal opportunities at work and equal pay, to mention just a few. Although such laws are very necessary, they have made the whole process of employment more complex. This has been necessary to protect employers as well as employees. The importance attached to the rights and obligations of employers and employees today is a comparatively new phenomenon. Indeed, up until the introduction of various Acts of Parliament to govern employment, employees had few rights at all. Listed below are just a few of the laws which have been introduced in the last three decades (see also Appendix 2):

1969   The Employers Liability (Compulsory Insurance) Act
1970   Equal Pay Act
1974   Health and Safety at Work Act
1975   Sex Discrimination Act
1976   Race Relations Act
1978   Employment Protection Act
1984   The Data Protection Act
1984   Trade Union Act
1986   Wages Act
1990   The Employment Act

These laws have introduced rules, regulations and minimum standards which employers and employees must adhere to. Clearly, this has placed a much larger workload upon those people within an organisation who are concerned directly with the wellbeing of the workforce. In the past, what would have been the responsibility of just one or two individuals is now divided between whole departments, called personnel departments, or more often nowadays, human resource departments. Even small and medium-sized businesses employ people to oversee their personnel practices, or hire the help of external consultants to advise them on the law and recruitment practices.

One other factor has increased the role of the personnel practitioner: the fact that people generally stayed in the same job for life was mentioned earlier, but the situation is very different today. It is estimated that each person has an average of five job changes throughout the course of his or her working life, and that number is increasing steadily. Indeed, with the increased employment prospects anticipated by the single European market the number of individual job changes is set to increase still further, as mobility between the professions in the European Community is encouraged. The impact of these changes will be felt most strongly by personnel departments who are in the front line of recruitment. For instance, as one person leaves an organisation, another person has to be recruited to fill the vacancy. The workload involved in this one single move includes at least five steps:

1 Advertising a vacancy
2 Personnel specification forms and job descriptions
3 Short-listing and interviewing
4 Selecting the best person for the job and sending out letters of rejection to the other applicants
5 Induction programme for the new employee

And not to forget all the other administrative tasks such as making changes to the payroll, pension scheme, bonus records, and the transfer of the previous employee's documents to his or her new firm. So it is clear that as employees expectations have increased and the range of available jobs has grown, the amount of information and range of skills needed in a personnel department has also expanded. Although new technology and the expertise of computers can assist the administrative tasks they cannot in themselves assist human relations, the central task of personnel departments.

THE DEVELOPMENT OF HUMAN RESOURCE MANAGEMENT (HRM)

The term 'human resource management' has partly grown out of the term 'personnel management'. It has been coined in response to the wider range of personnel tasks which has recently developed. It has also come about in response to the growing awareness that it is an organisation's workforce which represents its most valuable asset.

Traditionally, it was widely believed that the personnel function was primarily about hiring and firing staff. However, it is now acknowledged that the role includes a whole range of other tasks associated with employer and employee relations: recruitment, training and promotion, career development, retention of key staff, lay offs, redundancy and retirement, to mention just a few. These, combined with the more established personnel tasks, such as grievance and disciplinary matters, negotiations with trade unions and staff associations, and the general welfare of staff, demand an enormous amount of expertise and knowledge within personnel departments in the 1990s. The tasks involved in human resource management therefore can be seen to be far more wide-ranging than previously imagined; and the role of the human resource manager is now acknowledged as a central part of running a successful organisation.

In the last few years, much greater emphasis has been placed on the fact that business is all about communication between people, and that business success relies heavily on the conditions being right at work to enable people to work to their full potential. This interest in the workforce, as well as in the products and services an organisation manufactures and delivers, has made the role of human resource professionals much more significant. Planning and preparation have become two of the major tasks of the human resource department. This means planning not only current tasks in respect of the existing workforce, but also planning ahead and taking into account these two points:

• What future personnel requirements may be necessary in light of the company's future aims and objectives? A comprehensive business plan can assist in forecasting these needs.
• What type of skills are needed, and does the current workforce match these skills?

EXERCISE

Look through national newspapers at advertisements for personnel or human resource managers. What sort of job description is provided in the advertisement? If possible, send away for a range of personnel specification forms and job descriptions. These should give you an idea of the vast amount of responsibility which these jobs entail. In addition, talk to people you know who are involved in these departments at work: what are their major tasks? To find out more, you could carry out a job study. This might involve asking questions under the following headings:

- What are the key tasks involved in the job?
- What are the secondary or subsidiary tasks?
- What sort of personal qualities and characteristics are suitable for the job?
- What is the work environment like?
- What are the likes and dislikes associated with the job? (Clearly, this will differ between individuals, but a pattern might still emerge.)
- What are the promotion prospects and opportunities for career development?

This should enable you to build up a picture of a typical day in the career of a personnel professional. Of course, because the job is all about people, a typical day is probably very difficult to define. To find out more about the variety of tasks which come under the personnel role, visit the local careers office or library for more information about this type of work.

The move away from personnel management to human resource management is evident in the growing number of advertisements for human resource managers. Indeed the complexity and variety of the human resource management role is evident within the chapters of this book, all of which are concerned with some aspect of HRM.

Employing people is rarely a simple matter, and retaining good staff can also be a problem. Regardless of the nature of a business, whether a large private company or a small charitable organisation employing a handful of staff, an employer has certain rights and obligations to his or her employees. By establishing good employment practices at the beginning, a company will not only be reducing possible areas of disagreement, but will also be acting responsibly towards one of its most important assets: its employees. Quite often, bad practices lead to low morale and conflict, which can be an unnecessary and wasteful drain on time and money. Having to constantly recruit because of high staff turnover is just one sympton of this.

So, managing people has become a central business activity. Old style management techniques which relied heavily on strict control and which seldom considered the employees, have been replaced by greater flexibility in working practices and increased cooperation between management and employees. Time and money is now pooled into developing good staff relations, for the long-term benefit of employers and employees alike. A highly-trained workforce is now regarded as playing a major part in the success or failure of a firm. In turn, this has placed staff welfare and training high on the agenda of HRM departments.

MAJOR INFLUENCES ON THE LABOUR MARKET IN THE 1990s

Changes in wider society are reflected in the workplace and the labour market. The workplace is simply a microcosm of society. The whole of industry represents an important part of society and is influenced by all economic, social and political changes that are happening at any particular time. It is in this context, therefore, that both employers and employees cannot afford to ignore events in the community beyond the workplace as the risk of ignorance involved would, in the end, affect the success or failure of any enterprise. Significant changes in wider society will inevitably affect decisions made by employers. The emphasis on the economic influence of the single European market, for example, ought not to be overlooked by employers, since it will affect the futures of both traditional local workforces as well as the larger European workforce. The belief that a comprehensive recruitment policy is essential is widespread and frequently voiced. It is, however, notoriously difficult to put into practice, since it requires a wide range of coordinated measures in such sectors as training, induction, marketing, advertising, information and finance, to mention just a few.

Implementing such a policy means taking into account not only the regulations governing the activities of economic measures, such as legal measures on trade, tariffs (a list of duties or customs to be paid on imports and exports), and tax laws, but also relies heavily on effective human resource management. In short, HRM is about the people involved and the relationships between them.

DISCUSSION POINT

Put simply, organisational behaviour is about human beings and their relationships with each other and with the company as a whole. If an organisation employs, for instance, 150 people, that means 150 entirely different personalities with different needs and a wide variety of experience. What external influences does each person bring to his or her work? Try to list as many as you can. For example, concerns over children, education, money, health, transport, travelling long distances.

The European Community is acutely aware of the role the human factor plays for all our nations in world economic competition. Much thorough and painstaking study and experience has led to the conclusion that human resource management, with its many aspects, is a specialist field in its own right. In light of this, the European Commission has introduced several human resource programmes to increase its commitment to the career development of Community citizens.

Effective recruitment is the most profitable means by which firms may gain a competitive advantage, because if the right recruitment decisions are made, the right job performance will follow. It does, however, involve a great many risks, and these have to be tackled as rationally as possible by personnel managers and human resource professionals. European firms will never get ahead of their rivals, particularly the Americans and the Japanese, unless large numbers of them make a firm resolve to recruit and select employees in an organised method within a well-planned framework. The Community's member states are aware of this problem and some have well-established support systems. For instance, the national careers service network in the UK offers employers a route to obtaining personnel, albeit almost exclusively young people. The Commission's best line of approach is not to duplicate what already exists in member states, but to devise other systems. The main aim behind any EC strategy is twofold:

- to give a practical boost to professional mobility in the European Community;
- to encourage the exchange of good practice within the larger European market, and partnerships between firms in different countries. Partnerships or twinning organisations can rotate staff periodically, and can exchange information and expertise in their fields. This can form a lasting bond and a worthwhile economic investment.

EXERCISE

Find out if there are any firms in your area which have twinned with other European organisations. This information might be available from your chamber of commerce, or from one of the European Information Centres (EICs), who might keep lists of companies which are involved in one of the EC's exchange programmes. Arrange to visit one, and present a summary of your discussion to your group.

Recruitment policies, like equal opportunities policies, are successful only in the long term, since programmes which offer overnight solutions are impossible to sustain for any length of time. The action taken within organisations in respect of recruitment and selection decisions is now more important than ever; the single market of 1992 means that large firms in all member states must be able to cooperate in recruitment and personnel management. Experts in all relevant professions must know each other, work together, and apply their skills throughout the community.

Underlying all of the EC's principles of transnational mobility and recruitment, are methods and practices that can be taught, together with the external influences which ought not be overlooked; the rationale behind this chapter. In the end, the ability to cope with change and stay ahead in enterprise is vital when competing on a world scale. The diagram below shows some of the major influences in the labour market and organisations in the 1990s. Some of these influences are discussed here.

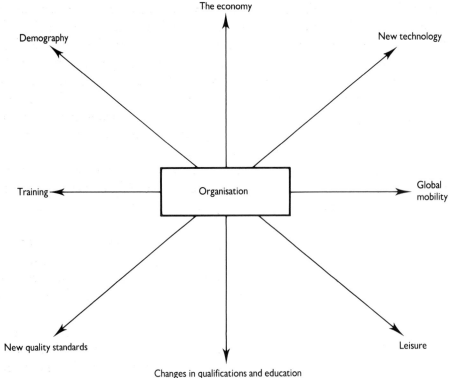

DEMOGRAPHY

This is about the population, which in turn is about people; the numbers of people in a country at any given time. Demographic changes influence the make-up of the labour market. A classic example of this was Germany after the Second World War, when large numbers of men were killed or went missing. This resulted in many more women than men being involved in the German labour market, even in the construction and engineering industries which had previously been traditional male strongholds. Wars play a major role in influencing a country's population.

EXERCISE

In terms of population figures, the EC is made up of both small and large countries. Listed below are the 12 members of the European Community. Approximate population figures are provided in brackets below. Try to match each country to its approximate population:

Belgium	Ireland	Greece
Luxembourg	Denmark	Portugal
France	Netherlands	Italy
UK	Spain	Germany

(360,000, then, in millions: 55.5, 10, 38, 78, 5, 10, 54.5, 14, 3.5, 55.5, 58)
Check your answers in an encyclopaedia or atlas.
What is the total approximate population of the European Community?

The decline in the birth-rate since the 1960s has had a major impact on the populations of all EC member states. The availability of contraception since the 1960s has given more women the opportunity to control when, or if, to have children, and how many children to have. One of the most significant effects of this has been the enormous increase of women in paid employment outside the home. In fact, with the massive redundancies which have taken place in traditional male dominated heavy industry, it is estimated that by the year 2000 women will be the dominant sex at work. Clearly, current employment and economic structures will have to reshape the male power base in order to reflect this changing structure.

With the decline in the birth-rate there has been an obvious fall in the number of school leavers. It is not surprising therefore that the bulk of the labour market now consists of older workers. However, although this is clearly the case, and shall become even more so in the years ahead, little attention is being given to this issue within the corridors of power. In fact, the world of work is still heavily associated with the dominant youth culture which has prevailed since the 1960s. Youth have dictated the modes of fashion, style, music and leisure. Whole industries have built up to cater for the needs of young people, and have largely ignored the population aged over 40.

The number of young people available for work is set to decline by 30 per cent by the mid 1990s. Employment policies will need to change in order to cater for the entire workforce, and not just focus on school and college leavers. Fortunately, the process of change has already started in some quarters and several of the large Do-it-yourself shops and supermarkets have started to recruit older workers, and looked beyond the traditional school leaver as the primary source of recruitment. This broadening of recruitment structures will have to be followed by a great many other organisations, if the much talked about 'demographic time-bomb' is not going to explode in the face of short-sighted personnel departments. During 1988 and 1989, the Commons Employment Select Committee looked at the employment patterns of the over-fifties. The Committee was so disturbed by its findings that it suggested to the Trades Union Congress and the Confederation of British Industry that they should mount a joint campaign to challenge discrimination against older workers. A campaign to ban age discrimination in recruitment has been launched by the Alliance Against Ageism. The campaign focuses on the need to outlaw the use of upper age limits in recruitment advertising. The 1980s were a decade when the yuppy ruled and youth was king. Perhaps in the 1990s some recognition will be taken of age and experience.

EXERCISE

Organisations such as B & Q, Tesco and Sainsbury's have been praised by the Government for recruiting older workers. Try and find out which companies in your area take account of the issues concerning age in their equal opportunities policies, and are actually taking some form of action to attract older workers. Next, write an essay entitled 'Age discrimination in employment – a waste of human resources'.

An ageing workforce is likely to be a permanent feature of the European workforce for at least the next few decades. Increased lifespan, brought about by improved health and medical services has had an enormous impact on the quality of life for older people. The average life expectancy of both men and women has risen sharply this century, and is set to rise still further. As a consequence, the average number of older people who are willing and able to remain in active employment has also risen.

The shortfall in young people entering the labour market, and subsequent rise in older workers should not be regarded as a problem. Instead, it should be seen as an opportunity to change current recruitment ideas and practices. Similarly, the demise of Britain as a major manufacturing nation should not itself be cause for alarm. Rather it should be seen as an ideal opportunity for employers to turn their attention to the enormous amount of relevant experience and skills readily available among those previously considered not worth training because they were over 40 years old.

THE ECONOMY

In general, the supply of labour equals the number of people available to work. Demand equals the number of jobs available. When the demand for work equals the supply of work, recruitment should be a straightforward and simple process. However, with the continual effects of unemployment, this is rarely the case. Rarely, in fact, has there been a true picture of full employment.

DISCUSSION POINT

In your area, who are the major employers? Approximately how many people do they employ? Has this number risen or fallen in the last five years? What are the likely reasons for this?

Recruitment policies are probably the first to be affected within an organisation when there are dramatic external influences upon the workforce. When there are few jobs in an area, an employer can afford to be selective and be fairly unconcerned about his or her staff retention rate, since, with little job opportunity elsewhere, an employee is less likely to leave. Alternatively, when jobs are in abundant supply, the boot is to some extent on the other foot; large numbers of jobs increase an individual's choice and his or her ability to demand higher wages in exchange for labour, so the incentive to remain in an unsatisfactory job is not so great. Take Solihull, for instance, a relatively prosperous town in the Midlands. During the economic boom of the mid 1980s the town's careers service was full of vacancies, often from very worried employers who were concerned about attracting labour that would stay for any significant length of time. Many school leavers had a choice of two or three jobs to apply for. It is not surprising therefore that finding work and staying in a job for economic security is less important when there are plenty of jobs available. This dilemma highlights the need for effective recruitment policies both in times of economic growth and in a recession. If the full benefits of recruitment and selection methods are to be reaped, it is not enough to rely on methods which fail to take into account the effects of economic changes on the labour market.

GLOBAL MOBILITY

A lot of debate has taken place over the past few decades about Britain's 'brain drain', referring to the large numbers of highly qualified people who have left the UK labour market to work in other countries where their skills and experience are more highly valued. The single European market is likely to increase worker mobility as more people welcome the freedom and challenge of the wider market. Indeed, the EC is actively encouraging the exchange of professional workers between member countries, and is paving the way for standardisation in qualifications and harmony in previously restrictive trade and tariff practices.

DISCUSSION POINT

In the early 1980s the EC identified the problem of the lack of free movement of professional people between member states. It announced that many people were being held back simply because of differences in qualifications between countries, which meant that an accountant who qualified in the UK, for example, could not work in Italy because his or her qualification was not recognised outside the UK. To overcome this problem, and to enable people to move freely about the labour market the EC have introduced a directive (a community law), to ensure that although professional education and training may vary between member states, any fully trained professional in a given field is likely to have much the same knowledge as that of his or her equivalent in a different EC country.

List as many advantages as you can of a common professional standard for employers and employees in the EC.

The single European market will give more employees the opportunity to seek work outside traditional borders than ever before. Although it is difficult to forecast future trends with complete accuracy, it is likely that for today's junior school children the prospect of careers guidance and jobs will take into account job locations never dreamt of by their parents. The impact upon employers also should not be overlooked, for in order to recruit and retain suitable staff they will be forced to provide the most lucrative incentives. One advantage of this from the employee's perspective, will be increased pressure on employers to provide childcare services and organised breaks for parents so that the current problems associated with juggling family and career responsibilities should be reduced.

The 1980s saw an upturn in the numbers of foreign companies taking up residence in the UK. The majority were companies with origins in Japan, Sweden and the USA. Imported cultures inject difference and competition into the traditional labour market. At the same time, skilled personnel are drawn away from the existing manufacturing bases.

With the combined influences of increased European mobility and foreign participation in the UK economy, both employers and employees cannot afford to ignore the importance of foreign language skills. The ability to speak more than one language places employees at an advantage and gives an organisation a competitive edge in trading overseas. Recruitment policies have therefore to reflect the European bias of the single market and to look at linguistic skills. Employers, both large and small, will need to identify the skills required in the workforce to meet both the single market challenge and the prospect of an increasingly globally oriented workforce. As many potential employees are attracted to working abroad, organisations may have to adapt their recruitment policies and, if necessary, look beyond the UK for the type of people they wish to employ. A growth in world travel and the single European market has a direct impact on all sectors of business including:

- Marketing expertise
- Import and export administration
- Transport and distribution
- Personnel
- Research and development
- Quality control
- Education and training

EXERCISE

Imagine you are the personnel manager of a large organisation and have been given the task of finding a suitable trading partner in another EC country. Write a list of the tasks you will have to undertake in order to ensure that the project is a success. Find out if there are any organisations or contacts in your area which could assist you.

NEW TECHNOLOGY

The significance of new technology cannot be overemphasised, since keeping abreast of changes is important for both manufacturers and service providers. As advances are made in the field of new technology and automation, men and women are being given more opportunities to participate in the changes. Enabling individual employees to influence the methods of introducing new technology into a company relies on mutual cooperation more than any other factor, as the people who generate the new technology come to realise how much they depend on those expected to operate it. It cannot be denied that new technology has mechanised many jobs previously undertaken by people. Many people have either been made redundant or retrained to adapt to the new technology. In good companies, a little foresight coupled with a willingness to acquire different skills through a solid investment in training has prevented many redundancies.

The advent of new technology has had the most profound effect on the human factor within the world of work. If we agree that no single individual is irreplaceable, then we must also accept that in the context of new technology, some individuals (those whose jobs are more vulnerable to being taken over by new technology) are more replaceable than others.

EXERCISE

New technology has swallowed up many jobs, especially those jobs which relied heavily on mechanical processes. In the future, it is likely that even more jobs will be replaced by new technology. However, there has been much scaremongering along the lines of 'machines are taking over', 'new technology is killing people's jobs' etc, when in fact, very many jobs, for instance, hairdressing, counselling, human resource management, training, teaching, performing arts – which are based on person to person contact – can never be replaced by new technology. There are many more jobs which can only be assisted by new technology, for example, careers guidance, personnel management, medicine, recruitment and selection, publishing, advertising, journalism, health and safety officers, retail and distribution.

First, make a list of the positive effects of new technology on people's jobs. Next, write a list of the points which you consider are the negative effects of new technology on the world of work.

In order to cope with the increasing effects of new technology in employment, many fair-minded and far-sighted employers have put a lot of effort into keeping their employees abreast of changes. Others have regarded the staff training, which is required to keep the workforce up to date, as an expensive and time-consuming luxury they can ill afford. It has, however, become very clear that those employers who have ignored the impact within the workplace of the 'technological revolution' have suffered, lost key personnel, and failed to be competitive, sadly with only themselves to blame. Without doubt, keeping up to date with new technology and new skills is an essential ingredient of business success. By reading the daily newspapers we are all painfully reminded of the fact that obsolete skills lead to business failures and redundancies.

Key trends in the labour market in the 1990s are likely to be in the continuing employment growth areas of highly skilled jobs, such as managerial, professional and technical jobs. These jobs both create and use new technology. They also generate a demand for higher level skills in the labour market. Overlooking the necessity of such skills in recruitment planning could cost employers dear.

REHABILITATION TECHNOLOGY

This is technology which is designed to enable people with disabilities to gain access to the workplace and to work effectively within it. For example, alterations to premises and the provision of suitable equipment, such as stair-lifts, hoists and closed circuit television. Enormous changes have taken place over the last 40 years in this field, which have enabled more and more people with disabilities to take their place in the world of work alongside able-bodied employees.

EXERCISE

How much has rehabilitation technology influenced the design of the building you are in at the moment? For example, are there many electric wheelchairs in use to increase mobility among students with physical disabilities? Stair-lifts, hoists, ramps, and ground-floor sanitary and kitchen facilities are just some of the facilities which have enabled disabled workers to integrate into employment more easily. Find out what else is available, and also what still needs to be done to enable people with disabilities to gain access to buildings in your area.

The crucial importance of equal opportunities for employees with disabilities in recruitment policies needs to be addressed much more so than in the past. Disabled workers form a particularly disadvantaged group. Very often, in fact, disabled people do not reach the final stages of recruitment as they are rejected from the very start, usually due to the employer's assumption that an individual with a disability is incapable of doing a job well. There is a pressing need for far more organisations to address disability issues, together with the advantages of rehabilitation technology, if the needs and abilities of this group are to be recognised and acted on. In the long term, tapping into the potential of unemployed disabled people is to the advantage of both employers and employees alike.

NATIONAL VOCATIONAL QUALIFICATIONS (NVQs)

Qualifications at all levels have undergone a massive process of reorganisation. Ordinary level and CSE examinations have been replaced by the national curriculum and GCSEs. These have largely demolished the traditional barriers between pass or failure grades. So, what have these changes meant for employers in seeking to recruit the best people for their organisations? Changes in secondary school qualifications have had the most effect on those employers who have traditionally targeted the school leaver market as their main recruitment source. Job descriptions, application forms, and interviewing skills have had to adapt to the changes which have taken place in mainstream education. It has placed increased emphasis on the need for industry and education to work more closely together in order to make the transition from school to employment simple for everyone concerned.

DISCUSSION POINT

Not only has the qualification system changed but the range of subjects on offer in schools and colleges has changed too. List all the subjects which can be studied in schools today. Talk to someone who left school 10 years ago, and, if possible, someone who left 20 years ago; how has the subject choice changed?

The traditional post-sixteen 'A' level qualifications have been joined by other types of less academic and more practical qualifications. A trend away from purely academic examination courses has occurred through the successful introduction of vocational courses such as BTEC, TVEI, NVQs, SVQs and more recently GNVQs. It is generally agreed that vocational courses equip students better than purely academic courses for many types of employment. These changes, however, have not been introduced without some opposition, from employers, parents, and politicians. Criticism has been levelled at the amount of confusion which has been created by large numbers of 'broadly equivalent' qualifications. Needless to say, staff involved in interviewing job applicants have had to keep up to date with changes in education. But for the employee with a new range of marketable skills and qualifications, his or her marketable capacity has soared.

Employers have a duty to keep up to date with changes in qualification structure; if only to ensure that the people they recruit are indeed the most appropriate for their type of organisation. NVQs have placed a responsibility on employers to ensure that, wherever possible, training and the achievement of qualifications is an on-going process and not a one-off event. A well-qualified workforce is beneficial to the whole organisation, as well as to individual employees. With the increased range of qualifications in mind, a business has to plan its training schemes in order to anticipate future demands. More qualifications mean more choice and flexibility for an employee, in adapting to his or her expectations of the labour market. Such choice should act as a warning to employers to ensure that they offer only the best in terms of induction and training programmes to all their employees and potential employees, so that they reap the benefits of a well-trained workforce and do not lose key staff to other organisations.

The single European market will affect the mobility of workers and the recruitment practices of employers. A number of measures are already in place to standardise qualifications and to make way for mutually compatible requirements throughout the EC. In the past, individuals who wished to migrate from one country to another, very often had to retrain in their new country. Nowadays, EC legislation exists to make it simpler for people to meet vocational training requirements between member countries. For several occupations, a job description has already been agreed by the EC which contains those elements common to all EC member states. A member country will issue a Certificate of Experience to a worker who meets the requirements of the EC directive covering his or her profession. In practice, this means that an individual can work in any of the 12 member states since a certificate will be accepted in place of their own national qualification for that job. Needless to say, employers who wish to recruit highly skilled people and maintain existing key staff need to ensure that they both offer and meet the requirements of qualification standards in the 1990s.

LEISURE

The role of leisure activities has increased in significance. As a result, a whole industry has been built around the real and perceived leisure needs of a predominantly youth culture. While the young are likely to be as preoccupied with training as with leisure, the growing numbers of retired people will naturally be more concerned with lifestyle and leisure.

But what effect has the much talked about 'leisure society' really had on the workforce and upon employers recruitment policies? In the 1970s, the much talked about three-day week never actually arrived. The high levels of unemployment in the 1990s highlight the need for alternative pastimes employing leisure services.

However, services must be provided free of charge if they really are to address the needs of the unemployed.

D ISCUSSION POINT

Find out what discounts are available in your area to enable unemployed people in the community to take advantage of leisure facilities. Make a list of leisure activities which are available at a discount or free of charge, and another list of expensive leisure interests. Due to the expense involved, how much leisure activity is really out of bounds for someone who is unemployed or on a very low income?

A change in traditional working arrangements to include flexitime, homeworking, temporary contracts and term-time only contracts, will enable more people to 'save' time in order to have more time for activities away from work. These developments in large organisations towards balancing employment time with private time ought to be reflected in employers' recruitment policies. If large numbers of employees wish to maximise leisure time, employers will have to be prepared to be more flexible than they have been in the past. These trends towards increased individual freedom will mean that employers shall have to examine their recruitment and induction methods, to truly reflect the changes in labour market trends.

Without doubt, each and every manager intent on recruiting key staff wishes only to recruit the best possible. However, key personnel with the best skills will now be in demand by numerous employers both in the UK and the wider European market. So it is important to consider, wherever possible, the inclusion of perks in order to recruit the best people for the job. In large organisations it might be appropriate to include in-house leisure facilities, such as a club or swimming pool, or provide financial discounts for staff to use local leisure services as part of the perks package.

Whatever impact the increased emphasis on leisure has on employment and the labour market, it does not alter the fact that for many employers their main recruits in future will be older workers. The future worker will be closer to statutory retirement age than school-leaving age. In fact, he or she may well be a retrained retired worker. Such employees, with decades of work experience and relative financial security behind them, will need to find the prospect of paid employment an attractive one. Employers will not be in a position to recruit and lay off as they see fit, but will have to provide lucrative packages in order to recruit and keep important staff. Many staff will possibly demand more consideration from their employers in such areas as flexible hours, increased holiday entitlement and social facilities. Employers will have to respond accordingly if they are to recruit and maintain the necessary staffing levels successfully.

D ISCUSSION POINT

A growing number of organisations, for example, Jaguar Cars, have successfully combined work and leisure activities by means of an on-site social club, swimming pool and sports teams. How else might businesses combine work and leisure activities? What are the advantages to the employer and employee of these arrangements?

QUALITY STANDARDS

The Kitemark has existed for over 60 years as an indication that a product conforms to a recognised British standard. During this time it has become one of the world's most widely recognised independent certification marks. The Kitemark of the future will increasingly be based on European standards (dual numbered as British standards). A quality mark acts as a passport for products allowing them to cross boundaries within the Community.

Quality is a more frequently talked about issue today than it was in the past. Indeed, all businesses are becoming increasingly quality conscious. Depending on the country of origin of a product, customers automatically have a number of prejudices, either for or against it.

DISCUSSION POINT

Think of the products which you have bought in the past: clothes, toys, games, jewellery, cars, electrical appliances, to mention a few. Sum up your feelings about various countries of origin such as Hong Kong, Taiwan, Japan, Korea, the USA, France and the UK. Does the country of origin influence your purchase?

New products are even more subject to these kind of judgements, and are often more open to criticism than their longer established competitors. A demand for greater consistency has led to the development of common standards in production, and much greater emphasis on quality over and above quantity.

In 1979, it was decided that a British standard for quality should be introduced. A standard was issued in 1979, and given the title BS5750. An updated version was introduced in 1987, which is dual numbered for international acceptance as ISO, the international standard, 9000. BS5750 is identical with ISO9000, so a company which is BS5750 registered, is recognised abroad. In practice, BS5750 registration means that a quality management system is in place, which is designed to maximise a company's performance in delivering the quality of goods or services expected, on the date required, at the price agreed, first time, every time.

EXERCISE

Look through recent copies of local newspapers. In the education pages, try to find what courses are available in your area for employers to achieve the BS5750 award. Also, contact any training organisations which run courses on BS5750 to find out the costs to local employers. Next, in the job advertisements, check to see if any employers are announcing their commitment to quality by mentioning that they have been awarded BS5750.

In light of the single European market, national requirements can actually prove to be a negative barrier to trade when they differ between member states. They can prove even more so, when governments and businesses do not recognise each other's methods for testing and certifying products. Nowadays, more than ever before, there is a need to agree on a single standard which is recognised right across

Europe so that businesses can operate, compete and cooperate successfully.

According to Freud, creativity is more important than productivity from the point of view of delivering a good quality service. This is particularly relevant to the wider European market where manufacturing processes are gradually being directed away from quantity and productivity, towards quality and creativity. The crucial commercial importance of providing high quality products in a competitive world goes without saying. Entrepreneurial success has always been bound up with the need to provide customers with a satisfactory product, something businesses can find costly. With the onset of the single market, tougher competition will force companies to make better use of their human resources in order to boost output. Improving the quality of work processes and involving the whole workforce in quality control decisions has a positive impact on the entire field of business activities, including:

- the design and quality of products;
- the fostering of mutual cooperation;
- the improvement of the working climate;
- the provision of staff with the opportunity to inject their own creativity and ideas.

Each of these factors helps to increase a company's chance of market success.

So, what has quality control got to do with recruitment and selection? If organisations want to derive the full benefit from any existing or future quality control method, a lack of clarity and thoroughness in recruiting appropriate staff could lead to problems in maintaining the desired standards. Quality working practices, either those which are laid down internally or imposed by national laws, demand many specific skills and expertise, for example:

- familiarity with local and international practice in specific business sectors;
- methods of design;
- methods of payment;
- research and development.

However, it is often a weakness at the recruitment stage which reduces the chance of smaller firms succeeding in maintaining high quality levels, because the ability to think 'quality' and operate effectively are just as crucial as any technological skill. So it is equally important that a new recruit cannot only contribute to the manufacture of a product, but that he or she is willing to take responsibility for the quality of the final product. The introduction of new improved quality standards means that quality control is nowadays regarded as a key factor in industrial development.

TRAINING ENTERPRISE COUNCILS (TECs)

TECs were established throughout England in 1989 and 1990. They are business-led organisations which provide a local focus for training through the planning and delivery of Government training schemes. They are also involved in the promotion of other training and enterprise programmes within their localities. Training the workforce is crucial if companies are to maximise the benefits of operating within a single European market. Therefore, training has to be seen as an important component of any recruitment and employment policy.

Some of the issues that the TEC network is involved in throughout the UK include:

- Equal opportunities
- Special needs
- Investors in People programme
- Leadership skills
- Management skills and the Management Charter Initiative
- Adult training
- Youth training
- Training and enterprise programmes
- Career development loans
- Local training awards
- Establishing business clubs in major towns
- Strengthening careers advice to all young people
- Improving the relevance and quality of employer placements for young people
- Establishing helpline and counselling services for returners to the labour market

TECs can help employers meet the challenge of the single market in several ways. A number of TEC measures are about assisting small and medium-sized local businesses to recruit and train key staff, and to develop successful partnerships with European businesses through cross channel training programmes. Taking advantage of the single market or defending an existing reliable customer base will no doubt raise crucial questions about the future of businesses, whether they are established international successes, or newcomers eager to take on the challenge of trading overseas. Whatever the business, it could well demand a major rethink of how a firm can secure its future recruitment needs.

At the heart of all business processes in the 1990s, the TEC network connects the entire business environment. Promoting and stage managing economic enterprises has rapidly become a central feature of the TEC movement. In fact, by educating more of the workforce in business skills, the TECs are providing the future captains of industry. TECs are ideally suited in helping both employers and employees to master the industry/education interface, since they are kept continually up to date by central government on developments in employment and education. Above all, they put the competitive stance of firms into context by showing how to target appropriate recruitment policies and practices.

In the current climate of increased competition within the single market, the work of the TECs will play a major part in the continued success of many companies. Any business venture is fraught with risk, since original and competitively priced products are in themselves hard to come by and often fail when launched on the market. One of the main reasons for such failure is the difficulty of matching new products to the market. A product is even more likely to be unsuccessful if wrong recruitment decisions have been made. The employees involved may lack the necessary skills to sell, promote, market, innovate, experiment, etc. Unfortunately, it is often the case that the final product is too late or inappropriate for its intended market. This matching phase between products and people is the central role of the TECs in the whole process of commercial activity.

EXERCISE

Find out about the local TEC in your area. What services, courses, and business information does it provide for local businesses? If possible, arrange for someone from the TEC to visit your group to give a talk about the role of the TEC, and the range of services it provides for local industry. You may find out that it runs a business club for junior managers or, if it doesn't, you could conduct a market survey among local employers to see if it should introduce one.

TECs can assist companies in decisions about staffing structures so that they get it right from the beginning, before any expensive mistakes are made. Also, shortcomings or mismatches between skills required and skills available can be overcome through training courses delivered locally by TECs. They may also be useful in keeping companies up to date on national laws and new national and European regulations. Through retraining staff and training new staff, TECs can improve an employee's usefulness within an organisation. Several TECs provide specific training courses with an inter-European bias. These courses will equip both employers and employees to work effectively with other European businesses. Foreign language training is also being encouraged through the TEC network, to assist business communication between member countries. Eventually, recruitment methods and recruits will be increasingly motivated by language skills needed for inter-trading. A multitude of languages amongst staff within a company will help enormously in the rapid breakdown of business information from a wide range of international origins and sources.

PLANNING A SUCCESSFUL RECRUITMENT CAMPAIGN

As we have seen, demographic changes, skill shortages, and the drop in the number of school leavers entering the labour market mean that recruitment methods can no longer be left solely to chance. In the past, finding a job at 15 or 16 and remaining in it for life was common practice. Today, the majority of employees change jobs much more frequently and only a very small number stay in the same job for their entire working lives.

Recruitment planning aims to maintain and improve the ability of an organisation to achieve corporate goals. In turn, this enhances the contribution of every single member of the workforce. In simple terms, it makes sense to employ people whose skills will be fully utilised, and who will be provided with satisfying work in the context of controlled costs. This prevents unnecessary overtime, and also avoids people being allocated to jobs for which they have not been trained.

THE NATURE OF HUMAN RESOURCES

One doesn't need to be a sage or a genius to appreciate that every person is unique, nor to understand that an organisation needs specific people able to do specific jobs. The main human resource factors which need to be taken into consideration include:

- matching the workforce available with job requirements, in order to prevent a surplus of people becoming a drain on profits;
- the difficulty of transferring people to other departments;
- recruitment planning should be a continuous exercise, taking account of current and future skill requirements and staffing requirements.

Recruiting new staff presents an opportunity for every manager to influence future business success. Apart from traditional approaches to recruitment and training, many employers are now introducing a range of specific measures to ensure that continuous improvements are made, such as women returner courses, work shadowing and work exchanges. This helps to achieve a multiskilled workforce with transferable skills.

It is important to identify the skills required within the workforce required to meet the single market challenge, and the needs of the ever-widening world economic market. It is likely that in future, recruitment policies may need to change still further and look beyond traditional sources of recruitment such as the school-leaver market, and if necessary to look beyond the UK for the right people. Some key questions which will need to be addressed include:

- Is human resource planning built into the main business objectives, and is there a proper strategy?
- Has the company got the internal resources to compete in the single European market?
- May we acquire new skills by training our existing workforce, or by recruiting extra staff with new skills?

DISCUSSION POINT

What do you see as the 'people problems' which would have to be identified and overcome when a firm decides to trade beyond its immediate locality and do business in the single European market?

HUMAN RESOURCE PLANNING

Care and thought in recruitment enables an employer to improve the performance of his or her company, and also provide the basis for putting into action any future objectives. When newly recruited personnel managers take over an existing section, they have little option but to take people as they find them and do their best to improve performance. When a personnel manager is recruiting new staff, the position is entirely different, and there is a much greater degree of choice as to:

- Who to recruit
- Why?
- What gap they will fill and what their role will be
- When the most appropriate time is to launch a recruitment campaign. (Does it fit in with the rest of the company's activities in the business calendar?)

SKILLS ANALYSIS/AUDIT

Matching the skills available in the workforce with those which may be required in future is an important activity for human resource managers. Skill shortages create problems in the labour market when the available stock of people with certain skills is not meeting the current or anticipated demands. In practice, the term 'skill shortage' is often used to stress underlying labour market problems resulting from shortages in the qualifications and experience of employees, due to insufficient training and education. In terms of a country's economy, skill supply strategies are measures which are taken to bridge the gap between skills available and skills required. In terms of individual companies eager to recruit and retain the right staff with the right range of skills to meet current and future product and service demands, a skills analysis should be carried out. This is simply a means of assessing the existing range of skills in the workforce, together with the future needs of the company. This enables organisations to:

- understand skill requirements;
- plan and invest in human resources, training tools and technology;
- attract the right people with the appropriate skills.

DISCUSSION POINT

Make a list of the advantages of carrying out a skills analysis or skills audit. When should it take place, and how often?

METHODS OF RECRUITMENT

Any or all of the following methods may be used:

- Internal advertisements
- Press (local or national newspapers or trade journals)
- Minority newspapers, for example, *The Afro Caribbean Times*, and journals/ magazines aimed at older people or workers with disabilities
- Job centres
- The Placing, Assessment and Counselling Team based at the local job centre or employment service who hold details of workers with disabilities
- Youth Training or Adult Training centres
- Chance applicants
- Careers service
- Employment agencies
- Management consultants
- Recruitment agencies
- Temporary agencies
- Executive search (head hunters)
- Visits to schools, colleges, universities
- The higher education milk round
- Job clubs
- Careers conventions

EXERCISE

Imagine you have the following two vacancies to fill:
1 forklift truck driver
2 purchasing manager with background in accountancy
What do you think would be the best recruitment method for each vacancy?
Would it be better to advertise the vacancy locally, or might you consider a national advertisement? Visit the local library and consult a range of professional journals to find out the type of jobs advertised. Are the majority national or international?
Present the results of your research to your group either as a talk or a report.

THE JOB ADVERTISEMENT

Space allocation for job advertisements in newspapers is often quite small, since very few companies can afford a full page advert. Therefore, bearing in mind the space restrictions, what information should be included in a job advertisement? The following details should really be the minimum:

- the organisation's name and location;
- a job description, outlining the major duties;
- qualifications required;
- salary;
- benefits, such as company pension scheme or leisure facilities;
- technology used;
- important facts about the organisation, for instance, is it part of a multinational group which might involve relocation or foreign travel?

DISCUSSION POINT

Look through the situations vacant columns in local newspapers. Does every job advertisement provide all of the information which is outlined above? Are the details provided sufficient, or do you think more are needed? Make a list of the most common details which are absent from many of the advertisements.

EXERCISE

A   Advertising: conduct your own advertising campaign. Think of two very different jobs such as a secretary and a nuclear scientist and compile a list of five places where you could advertise each post in order to get the best response.
B   When your group has decided where to place the advertisements, discuss what kind of details ought to be included in the advertisement. Design a sample advertisement to include these details. Should certain key details stand out, such as wages, holidays, bonus schemes, special perks, major duties? If so, make them stand out by writing them in capital letters or italics; or, if you have access to a wordprocessor, highlight them in bold, or italics, or underline them.

APPLICATION FORMS

An application form is used by many organisations as the primary tool in selection. Application forms act as a useful preliminary to employment interviews and decisions. They enable interviewers to use the form as a basis for the interview, and make short-listing the best candidates easier.

In the last few years several organisations have lengthened their application forms in order for them to play a more useful part in the selection of candidates. Detailed application forms are a means of getting to know more about a candidate than can be provided in a half-hour interview. They also help candidates to present their case without the pressure of an interview situation, and they speed up the sorting and selection process. They can provide a starting point for personnel records, such as those kept on sickness, absenteeism, training courses attended.

PERSONAL DETAILS

In the past, and even today too in some organisations, application forms have asked a lot of questions about a candidate's personal circumstances, including:

- Marital status
- Number of children
- Ethnic origin

The application form is designed to enable the selection committee to find out about the candidates history. However, there is obviously a difference in a candidate's personal history and his or her employment history. Personal details can lead to subjective and inaccurate impressions being made which can lead to prejudice and discrimination in recruitment. After all, a person ought to be selected on his or her ability to do the job alone, not on any external details like childcare arrangements or irrelevant questions about marital status.

EXERCISE

In small groups, draw up a list of details which an application form ought to include. After you have thought of as many details as possible, place them in order of priority and group them under the following headings:

- Personal details
- Employment experience
- Education, schools, colleges and other training courses attended
- Educational qualifications
- Other qualifications
- Interests
- References

At this point think about how much space on the form should be allocated for each section. Also, should personal details be included in the main body of the form or on a separate sheet to be used only for the purposes of monitoring the equal opportunities policy? What are the implications of the two approaches from an equal opportunities point of view?

Now exchange forms between groups to compare and contrast how each group has ordered and grouped the information. If you like, award each form a score out of 10.

The whole group should now design an *ideal* form based on the best contributions from the sub-groups. It might be useful if you scan the local newspapers for job vacancies, and phone up to ask for an application form. Compare those you receive with your own recommendations. You may like to try filling them in yourselves to assess how easy or difficult it is.

JOB DESCRIPTION

This is the result of a careful job analysis and should include a detailed statement of all physical, mental and organisational aspects of the job. It should be sent out with application forms, and include a brief description about the department in which the applicant will be based.

HARGREAVES POLYTECHNIC

Job Title: Personnel officer for women students and staff

Faculty/Service: Women's Unit

Grade/Salary: Principal Officer £16,746 pro-rata

Job Description: General Responsibilities

- To work within the corporate aims of the Polytechnic and in particular to contribute to the promotion and achievement of Polytechnic policies as they relate to women.
- To establish effective communication, liaison and cooperation with faculties, services, staff and students.
- To prepare a plan of action, implementation strategy and produce progress reports.
- To promote an environment which will enable all women to reach their full potential.
- Monitoring and evaluation of the effectiveness of existing Polytechnic policies with regard to women's issues and initiating and participating in positive action programmes.
- To identify the social, employment, academic and welfare needs of all women in the Polytechnic.
- To propose new policies and developments where appropriate.
- To encourage and liaise with women's groups and networks within the Polytechnic.
- To identify and develop good practice with regard to women's issues.
- To develop external links including international contacts and networking with women's groups.
- To ensure that issues affecting women are explored, effectively addressed and included in course design, delivery and review.
- To encourage the development of research projects and income generating activities on women's issues
- To produce reports relevant to women's affairs, and make them available to other polytechnic services and departments, as well as to interested groups locally.
- To build and maintain a database of useful contacts
- Other activities as determined by the Rector or nominee.

Job Reference: NT/164A

Closing Date: 12 September 1994

0.6 of this post is currently filled and we are seeking to make an appointment for the remaining 0.4 on a job-share basis, working all day Thursday and Friday.

PERSONNEL SPECIFICATION FORMS

Personnel specification forms help employers to decide what type of person would ideally suit the job. Why do employers need a personnel specification? Simply because it is important to know what the person will contribute and what induction training will be required.

EXAMPLE

Job Title:	Personnel assistant
Faculty/Service:	Policy and Administration
Grade/Salary:	Principal Officer £12,345 to £14,786 depending on age, experience and qualifications

ATTRIBUTES	ESSENTIAL	DESIRABLE
Work experience	Working within a medium to large organisation Experience of personal involvement in dealing with women's issues	Policy Development and implementation work Experience of working within a higher/further education environment
Education/qualifications	Degree	
Skills/abilities	Knowledge of equal opportunities legislation and its implications for education	Presentation skills; self-motivating skills
	Report writing Networking skills Ability to liaise across the Polytechnic at all levels	
Personal details	Empathy with issues common within women's lives Commitment to equal opportunities and aims of the Mission Statement	

EXERCISE

A What are the main duties associated with these jobs: typist, salesperson, graphic designer, hairdresser, personnel officer? What skills does each job require? If you don't know, visit the local careers office to find out more about each job.

B Choose one of the jobs mentioned above and write out 10 points associated with it; five points should relate directly to the job itself which we shall call the job description; the remainder should relate to the skills needed in order to carry out the duties successfully, which we will call personnel specification. For example, a telephonist's main duties are answering the telephone and taking messages. To carry out these duties properly, a clear voice and a polite manner are important skills. The list you have compiled is what is known as a personnel specification form for a given job.

INTERVIEWING

Recruitment is an important managerial task because an employer may have to live with his or her decision for a long time afterwards. It is important to ask a number of questions about the job before any decision to advertise a vacancy or interview candidates is made, such as:

- Is this a long-term role?
- Can it be filled internally? If so, it ought to be advertised on internal noticeboards to comply with the equal opportunities policy.
- Does it demand any specialist knowledge or skills?
- Can it be merged with other responsibilities in order to make it a more attractive and interesting job?

The decision making and judgement of all candidates should wait until after all the interviews have taken place. The primary reason for the interview is to make the best match between the candidates interviewed and the job or jobs available. Candidates should be compared with the the job specification before they are compared with each other. Computerised selection methods have been devised whereby points are awarded for different factors, each candidate being scored individually, and the highest scorer being awarded the post. Computerised methods can be useful, but should never be used as the only method. The main advantages of computerised methods in assisting decision making are:

- they divide information into related sections;
- they encourage the interviewer to ensure that the information gathered is as complete as possible;
- they set out areas of information that are relevant to the employment decision, and avoid the human tendency to stray off the point.

In most cases an application form or a curriculum vitae for each candidate is available for the interviewing panel to read well before an interview takes place. Interviews are difficult and demanding because no two persons are alike. Some people express themselves better in writing than in conversation, and this factor has to be taken into account. Effective listening and well-timed open questions (see below) encourage honest responses.

TEN POINT PLAN FOR INTERVIEWING

1 Plan what needs to be covered in the interview, but be prepared to be directed by the candidate's responses and answers.

2 Take brief notes, do not rely on memory; it is very easy to mistake one candidate for another, especially if several people are interviewed in one day.

3 Invite the interviewees to take notes if they wish.

4 Get the interviewee to enlarge on the facts given on his or her curriculum vitae. The secret of successful interviewing is to get applicants to talk about themselves, so as to enable the interviewer to get to know as much about them in the time available.

5 Be alert to the interviewee's strengths and weaknesses.

6 Do not ask questions which produce only yes or no answers. Open questions which invite a long answer produce much more information.

7 Ask for career aims and future goals and compare them with a candidate's past experience.

8 Be sure that applicants have a chance to reveal all relevant information.

9 Allow candidates to question you and find out as much as possible about the job and the company.

10 Do not ask personal questions which arouse the suspicion in a candidate that you may be prejudiced against him or her. In order to comply with equal opportunities, always ask yourself, 'Would I ask this question of a man?' or 'Would I ask this question or make this assumption about a white person or an able-bodied applicant? As a general rule, always ask each interviewee the same questions.

After job interviews there is always a mass of information for the interview panel to evaluate. Each candidate needs to be compared with the others as well as examined on an individual basis to assess their suitability. Follow the interview by preparing a short list. Break down the candidates on the short list under the following headings:

EXPERIENCE
- What experience/opportunities have the applicants had?
- What positions of responsibility have they had?
- What decisions have they made?
- What results have they achieved?

MOTIVATION
- What career choices have the applicants had?
- What influenced them?
- What risks have they taken?
- What have they got out of their career, and what have they put into it?

ACHIEVEMENTS
- Have they done well in their career so far?
- What problems have they solved and what new ideas have they contributed?
- Were they supported or in a supportive role?
- Have they demonstrated that they could work on their own initiative?

All of this information can be obtained from some or all of the following sources:

- Application forms

- Interviews
- References and information obtained from past employers, schools or colleges
- Selection tests
- Work experience records

LETTERS OF REJECTION

Interviewing always involves electing winners and losers. In general there are far more losers than winners. A good interviewer will always select the best person for the job. Sometimes though, a candidate who narrowly misses a job would do well elsewhere in the organisation, and his or her details should be passed on to the appropriate department or to personnel to keep on file.

Once a decision has been made and a candidate has been selected, it is easy to forget the rest. Think about how often you have heard people say they have replied to job advertisements, attended interviews and not heard a word from the company since. This is bad management practice, since if candidates reply to advertisements and attend interviews, employers should have the courtesy to respond to all those who applied. Another point to remember is that organisations are dynamic: continual movement is dictated by the ever changing demands of the market and by people's desire to improve their careers. As an employer, a good company image is an important asset. A good image will not be maintained if the company behaves badly to applicants and potential employees.

DISCUSSION POINT

In your group, among those of you who have applied for jobs, either full-time, part-time or temporary posts, how often have group members not even received an acknowledgement from the company? Summarise your feelings towards the company when this has occurred.

The following points for letters of rejection should be considered:

- if there was a specific reason why the applicant was not suitable, perhaps mention the reason in the letter. This may enable the candidate to correct the fault or alter his or her behaviour in a future interview;
- word it gently, even rejections can be phrased in helpful and positive language;
- if time permits, try to write to each candidate personally rather than using a general rejection letter;
- all letters should be kept on file in the event of a failed applicant alleging that discrimination took place in the recruitment procedure.

RECRUITMENT AND SELECTION CAMPAIGN CHECKLIST

The following diagram shows the recruitment and selection process. The checklist below details the issues and activities to remember when planning a recruitment and selection campaign.

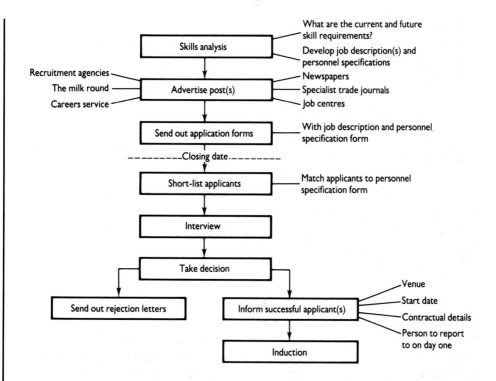

- Skills analysis/audit
- Sources of recruitment and recruitment methods
- Job advertisements
- Application forms
- Job specifications
- Personnel specifications
- Interviewing and short-listing
- Letters of rejection

FURTHER READING

Goodworth, C. T. *Effective interviewing for employment selection* Business Books Communica-Europa, 1979

Hayes, C. and N. Fonda, *Strategy and people: the prospect centre perspective* The Prospect Centre, 1988

McBeath, G. *Handbook of human resource planning* Blackwell, 1992

The IPM statement on human resource planning Institute of Personnel Management, 1986

EQUAL OPPORTUNITIES ISSUES

WHAT ARE EQUAL OPPORTUNITIES?

Equal opportunities are about treating each person fairly on the basis of individual need. It is clear though that each person's needs vary: a six-month-old baby, for example, has very different nutritional needs from a full-time professional hockey player. So they are not about treating each person the same, but are to do with treating everyone fairly according to his or her own special needs.

The two words most often heard in connection with equal opportunities are prejudice and discrimination. Prejudice is simply about making a prejudgement based on feeling rather than on fact. Because it is a prejudgement, it is often based on one-sided opinions which do not take into account any other viewpoints. Prejudice is linked to stereotypes: an image of a person or group of people which both creates and reinforces prejudice.

DISCUSSION POINT

1 What common stereotypes are used to describe groups of people?
2 Is it really possible to generalise with any degree of accuracy about whole groups of people, or are stereotypes based largely on fiction rather than on fact?

Discrimination is the action which is taken as a result of prejudice. It is probably true to say that we all harbour prejudices about all kinds of different groups of people. However, very few of us follow our prejudices through to actually discriminating against others. Equality of opportunity in the workplace aims to ensure that each person is able to reach his or her potential and is not held back by prejudice or discrimination. Put simply, prejudice is the thought process and discrimination is the action.

Employment laws have been introduced to protect the rights of employees and to ensure that employers provide minimum standards in such areas as pay, health and safety, pensions, holidays, sick-leave and maternity rights. The law on equal opportunities is designed to ensure that unfair discrimination does not happen in the workplace, and where it does happen, that the victim has the right to some form of compensation.

It should be noted that not all laws have traditionally sought to promote equality between people. Take slavery laws for example. It was not until 1833 that an Act of Parliament was introduced which abolished slavery in British colonies. More recently, in 1949 the South African government adopted the system of apartheid (separation of black and white) as official policy. Apartheid upheld a very unequal system, whereby white people had far more rights than the rest of the population. However, in the UK, as in the rest of Europe, the equality laws which have been introduced in the course of the last few decades are designed to promote equality of opportunity.

During the 1990s there is likely to be much more interest in equal opportunities. This is due to a number of different reasons. In 1991 a report published jointly by the government and the TUC showed that when the supply of 'baby boom' school leavers levels out during the 1990s, employers will need women to fill some 80 per cent of new jobs. The way this need can be met would be by bringing more women with dependent children into the workplace. It is interesting to note that in Britain, when women were needed for work during the Second World War, state nurseries were provided to cater for women with dependent children. These proved to be highly successful, but as soon as the war ended they were closed down and no government since has seen fit to revive them.

EXERCISE

Find out about the childcare options for the working parent which are available in your area. Also, which local companies have parent friendly policies such as childcare vouchers, creches or workplace based after school clubs. What is the average cost of childcare for two children in your area?.

During the past 20 years equal opportunities at work has become an increasingly important issue in employment, not only as a result of the introduction of laws to promote equal opportunities but also from a growing awareness that in order for the country to prosper, it needs to fully utilise its human resources. Equality laws exist to protect people against discrimination at work. Employers who wish to avail themselves of the widest pool of skills and experience, and offer their employees genuine equality of opportunity, have been persuaded to adopt equal opportunities programmes which go beyond the basic requirements of the law.

AN EQUAL OPPORTUNITIES POLICY

By declaring an organisation to be an equal opportunities employer, and taking pains to apply the principle, a company's image is considerably enhanced, and the likelihood of recruiting and retaining the best staff from the widest selection increased. Equal opportunities policies are more than a statement of good intention. Used properly, they provide a mechanism for avoiding management decisions based purely on prejudice, and offer all staff the chance to reach their full potential.

Keep a cross section of national and local newspapers for a month. Go through the job advertisements and find out how many are equal opportunities employers and how many claim to be working towards equality of opportunity?

An equal opportunities policy should include:

- a statement of intent to avoid discrimination, and to challenge it if, or when, it occurs;
- what it means in terms of recruitment, selection and promotion procedures;
- what it means in terms of training;
- how the policy will be monitored and who will be responsible for it.

The policy should also be accompanied by a series of training and awareness raising seminars for all staff, especially for those staff who are directly involved in recruitment and interviewing. If people are made aware of their responsibility to act in accordance with the policy, they are more likely to be committed to its aims and objectives. Training courses should emphasise that an equal opportunities policy is to the advantage of the entire workforce and not just a small handful of employees.

THE LAW ON EQUAL OPPORTUNITIES

The laws covering sex and race discrimination are designed to outlaw discrimination and promote equal opportunities. The Sex Discrimination Act was introduced in 1975, and the Race Relations Act in 1976. Employers must not discriminate against anyone on the grounds of sex or race by treating them less favourably in all aspects of employment, including recruitment, training and promotion. If they do, it is referred to as direct discrimination.

Examples of direct discrimination are:

- presuming some types of work are unsuitable for women or black people, and therefore only advertising a vacancy for men or white people;
- asking only women candidates at interview about their domestic commitments. A good rule to follow is to never to ask a woman any questions which you would not ask of a man;
- allowing male employees five weeks paid holiday and female employees three weeks.

There is a second form of unlawful discrimination, known as indirect discrimination. This occurs when a condition or requirement is imposed on everyone in the workforce, but which:

- is such that the proportion of women or the proportion of a particular racial group able to comply with it is much smaller than the number of men or white employees who can;

- the employer cannot show is justified;
- is detrimental to the individual or group concerned.

Examples of indirect discrimination include:

- setting unnecessary height requirements for a job, such as stating that all candidates must be over six feet tall. Clearly, this is a requirement which favours male candidates, and a much smaller number of women can comply with it than men;
- selecting staff by language tests or culturally biased aptitude tests. For example, requiring English language to GCSE grade C standard when the job could be adequately performed without this qualification, or asking general knowledge questions in a selection test which are entirely to do with British culture. Clearly, a lower proportion of recently arrived immigrants or people whose first language is not English could comply with these requirements;
- placing a job advertisement in an all-white catchment area.

D ISCUSSION POINT

How might a manager indirectly discriminate in the arrangements he or she makes to recruit more employees? Apart from directly restricting applications for the jobs to men, how might an advertisement be worded so that the job does in fact go to a man?

It is also unlawful to discriminate against men or women on the grounds of marital status, such as by:

- not recruiting married people for a job which involves being away from home;
- making only married rather than single people redundant.

It is also unlawful for employers to victimise any worker for pursuing a sex or race discrimination claim. Put simply, an employee who asserts his or her rights under one of the Acts of Parliament should not, by doing so, suffer further discrimination. Employees have the right to take a discrimination claim to an industrial tribunal regardless of how long they have been employed by an organisation. In fact, even potential employees who feel that they have been discriminated against in the recruitment process have a right to take a claim to a tribunal.

GENUINE OCCUPATIONAL QUALIFICATIONS (GOQ)

In certain circumstances, employers can show that there is a genuine occupational qualification which demands that applicants must be of a particular sex or race (but not married or single, the GOQ exception does not apply to discrimination on this basis). One important point to bear in mind in respect of the GOQ exception is that it does not apply where there are already sufficient employees to carry out the duties associated with the job. There are three more important points to bear in mind when establishing if the GOQ exception applies. These are:

- where a specific sex is required, for example, to preserve decency where a job involves personal contact such as in a female changing room at a public swimming baths;
- where a particular racial group is required to provide authenticity, for example, a Chinese restaurant may recruit only Chinese waiters and waitresses so that the atmosphere is authentic;
- for personal services which are involved in promoting the welfare of a particular racial group, a member of that racial group may be appointed under the GOQ exception.

EXERCISE

Examine the job advertisements in local and national newspapers. Are there any posts for which the employer has got an exception to the laws governing sex and race discrimination under a GOQ? (If so it will say so, probably at the bottom of the advertisement.) What is the nature of the jobs for which a GOQ exception has been used in the vacancies you have located?

Similarly it is legal to discriminate in favour of one sex if an educational or training opportunity is:

- in an establishment that was single sex before the Act came into force;
- to prepare women for jobs that are traditionally done by men, in order to give women an equal chance of competing for such jobs in the future;
- for women only to help women returners to employment after an absence from the paid labour market due to domestic responsibilities.

Using these exemptions a number of courses have been set up throughout the UK. These courses represent what is often referred to as positive action. The main aim of positive action courses is to reduce the effects of past discrimination. They may include women into management courses, women into engineering, science and technology and women returner courses. They generally have the following advantages:

- childcare facilities, such as an on-site nursery or a financial contribution towards the cost of childcare;
- hours and teaching methods which take childcare and the school day into consideration.

EXERCISE

Look through the education, training and job pages in local newspapers. Are there any similar courses available in your area? If so, contact them and find out what special arrangements they have made to encourage a high take up by local people.

The Race Relations Act also allows for positive action to be taken to undo the effects of racial discrimination. Positive action can therefore be used to promote equal opportunities. It covers a range of measures to encourage and train people for jobs in which their racial group is under represented.

SEXUAL HARASSMENT

There is no single definition of sexual harassment, and many people have very different views about what constitutes harassment. In the European Commission's Code of Practice, sexual harassment is broadly described as 'unwanted conduct of a sexual nature, or other conduct based on sex affecting the dignity of women and men at work'. The majority of people who are sexually harassed are women, but it can happen to men too. No one should have to put up with sexual harassment, and having a workplace policy to deal with the problem is the most effective measure an employer can take to avoid a complaint arising. For maximum impact, it is important for the policy statement to include the following information:

- what constitutes inappropriate behaviour at work;
- a clear statement that sexual harassment may be treated as a serious disciplinary matter;
- a statement that all employees have a responsibility to comply with the policy and to treat colleagues of both sexes with respect and dignity;
- an outline of the procedure on how to bring a complaint of sexual harassment to the employer's attention;
- an assurance that allegations of sexual harassment will be dealt with seriously and confidentially;
- an explanation that such behaviour may in some circumstances be unlawful.

In fact, in one case, *Porcelli v Strathclyde Regional Council*, the Scottish Court of appeal ruled that a woman who complained of sexual harassment had suffered sex discrimination. In this case, a woman was resented by two male colleagues who behaved badly towards her, with the intention of forcing her to apply for a transfer to another post, which she eventually did. Their conduct included personal insults, obscene language and suggestive remarks. She won her case against her employers under the Sex Discrimination Act. Since then, there have been an increasing number of sexual harassment cases under the Act covering a range of different kinds of behaviour, ranging from relatively minor to very serious. It should be remembered that under the Sex Discrimination Act, employers are not only responsible for their own conduct but are also liable for any discriminatory behaviour of their employees in the course of employment. Employers can escape such responsibility only if they can prove that they took steps to prevent the employee's behaviour. (To find out more about this case and others like it, refer to *Sexual Harassment in the workplace: a guide for employers*, the Department of Employment 1992.)

THE EQUAL PAY ACT 1970

The Equal Pay Act was introduced to abolish discrimination between men and women in pay and other terms of their contracts of employment. This includes payments for overtime, bonuses and piece-work as well as other conditions of work such as working hours, holidays and sick-leave entitlements. It was amended in 1983 to give workers the right to equal pay for work of equal value.

Experience has shown that it is not always easy to decide whether a claim falls under the Sex Discrimination Act or the Equal Pay Act. In general, if a woman is being paid less than a man for the same job, the claim comes under the Equal Pay Act. If the dispute is about the offer of a job then it will fall under the Sex Discrimination Act. The basic idea of the Equal Pay Act is that, built into the contract of employment is an equality clause. This means that all employees are guaranteed equal treatment in the same employment:

- where there is work which is the same or broadly similar to that of a member of the opposite sex. (Work which is broadly similar is called 'like work');
- where an employee's work is of 'equal value' to a different type of work done by a member of the opposite sex, in terms of effort, skills and decision making. For example, in one successful claim, a cook was able to compare her work with a painter. Although the jobs are clearly very different, the claim was based on the fact that the jobs were of equal value to each other and therefore should be paid similar amounts;
- if an employee's job has been rated the same as that done by a member of the opposite sex, under a proper Job Evaluation Study (JES). A JES is a careful assessment of the responsibilities and tasks involved in the two jobs being compared. A JES must be accepted by both parties, the employer and the employee, if it is to be valid for a case hearing at an industrial tribunal.

E XERCISE

In the UK, women still only earn approximately 70 per cent of what men earn. Ask six men and six women you know who are engaged in a variety of different jobs. If possible find out what their annual or weekly pay is. How many reasons can you think of why women should be earning only three quarters of men's earnings?

EQUAL PAY CLAIMS

Employees who feel they have been denied equal pay can apply to an industrial tribunal, which will decide whether they are entitled to equal pay. Any employee who wishes to pursue an equal pay claim can do so at any time during her or his employment, or within six months of leaving the employment. There is no minimum length of service before a claim can be pursued under the Equal Pay Act. If an employee's case is successful she or he will be awarded equal pay (or equal treatment if their claim concerns terms of their contract such as holiday entitlements, which do not relate to pay).

OPPORTUNITY 2000

The 1990s have been heralded the decade of opportunity for women. Women now represent 45 per cent of the workforce, but in spite of the equality laws which have been in place now for over two decades, the status of women in the workforce still lags far behind that of men. The facts speak clearly:

- women's average hourly earnings have remained at around 74 per cent of men's for the last decade. In 1992, a woman's average weekly earnings were £201.50, compared to £295.60 for a man;
- women represent less than two per cent of all top executive jobs;
- of the total number of managers in the UK, only 20 per cent are women.

It is clear therefore that there is still a long way to go before true equality between the sexes is achieved. Opportunity 2000 is a campaign launched in 1991 and supported by the Prime Minister. It was set up as a result of work carried out by the Women's Economic Development team under the charity *Business in the Community*. Its aims are not only concerned with getting more women into paid employment, but more importantly, improving the quality of work which women pursue. At its launch, over 60 of the UK's top employers joined the campaign, demonstrating their commitment towards improving the opportunities for women at work. The whole range of British industry was present at the launch including:

- Major high street banks and building societies
- Television companies
- Many of the UK's major high street retailers
- Most of the UK's recently privatised large employers

EXERCISE

Contact *Businesses in the Community* to find out about any organisations in your area which are involved in the Opportunity 2000 campaign. If possible, arrange to visit them to find out what measures they have introduced to promote equal opportunities for women in the workplace. Also, what effects is the campaign having on managers and employees alike?

THE GOVERNMENT COMMISSIONS

Two government commissions have been set up to put the Acts of Parliament into practice. The Sex Discrimination Act created the Equal Opportunities Commission (EOC), and the Race Relations Act set up the Commission for Racial Equality (CRE).

THE EQUAL OPPORTUNITIES COMMISSION

The EOC consists of between eight and 15 full or part-time Commissioners, all of whom are appointed by government. One of them is appointed by the Secretary to be chairperson and one or two others to be deputy chairpersons. The main office is in Manchester and there are regional offices in Wales and Scotland. The EOC is funded entirely by the Home Office.

The role of the EOC is:

- to work towards the elimination of sex discrimination in all its forms;

- to promote equality of opportunity between men and women and to help individuals with any questions or complaints about discrimination;
- to keep under review the working of the Sex Discrimination Act and the Equal Pay Act, and to make recommendations to the Government for improvements to the Acts if appropriate.

THE COMMISSION FOR RACIAL EQUALITY

The CRE is the only organisation which is empowered to provide legal aid at industrial tribunal hearings on cases of racial discrimination. The CRE is run by up to 15 Commissioners who are appointed by the government, and they may make recommendations for improvements to the Act whenever necessary. The head office is in London with five regional offices throughout the UK. The Commission publishes several leaflets on equal opportunities and the rights and obligations of employers and employees under the Race Relations Act.

The main duties of the CRE are:

- to work towards the elimination of racial discrimination;
- to promote equal opportunities and good race relations between people of different racial groups;
- to keep the working of the Race Relations Act under review.

MATERNITY RIGHTS

Maternity and childcare issues have undergone revolutionary changes in the past decade or so, and a whole new range of benefits and services has been introduced in various European countries. Maternity leave and parental rights are two of the most significant changes which have come about, although some countries have gone further than others and have introduced statutory rights for 'time off for family responsibilities'.

Maternity pay in Britain is lower than in most EC countries. Some countries – Germany, Greece, Holland and Portugal – pay full salary for the whole period of maternity leave. In the UK, only those women who have worked for the same employer for two years, or part-time for five years, get earnings-related maternity pay.

The Employment Protection (Consolidation) Act 1978 states that all pregnant women have paid time off from work no matter when they started their job or how many hours they work. They must also be given the opportunity to attend classes designed to help women to prepare for the birth of the baby and to attend the hospital or clinic. A pregnant employee should give her employer as much notice as possible of any time she may be absent from work. The employer is entitled to ask for a medical certificate as proof of pregnancy and to see her appointment card for the clinic.

Many EC member states offer more than the bare minimum, for example:

- Luxemburg and France offer special grants to pregnant women if they have regular medical examinations;
- Denmark provides fathers with two weeks paternity pay;
- Greece pays a lump sum to women who have late miscarriages.

The variety of systems in the member states makes direct comparisons rather difficult. All EC countries provide a statutory amount of financial support for maternity leave, but the level of this differs greatly.

In the UK, pregnant employees can claim four rights under the law.

1 The right not to be dismissed.
2 The right to time off for antenatal care.
3 The right to maternity pay.
4 The right to return to work after confinement.

Let's examine each of these rights in turn.

THE RIGHT NOT TO BE DISMISSED

This applies to all women who have worked full-time for an organisation for at least one year. However, the law states that a woman can be dismissed if she is incapable of carrying out her job properly or, because of health and safety provisions, there would be a breach of some other law if she continued to work. In such a situation, it is important that the management assess other types of work which may well be more suitable in the circumstances.

THE RIGHT TO TIME OFF FOR ANTENATAL CARE

This is any woman's entitlement as long as she continues to work. Any time taken off for clinic or hospital visits must be paid at the normal rate. No continuous length of service is required in order to take this time off. So an employee with eight months continuous service has the same rights as an employee with eight years service.

THE RIGHT TO MATERNITY PAY

To qualify for Statutory Maternity Pay (SMP) an employee must:

- have been continuously employed by an organisation for at least 26 weeks continuing into the 15th week before her baby is due. This 15th week is known as the qualifying week (QW);
- have average weekly earnings of not less than the lower earnings limit for the payment of National Insurance contributions;
- still be pregnant at the 11th week before her expected week of confinement (EWC);
- have stopped working for an organisation.

THE RIGHT TO RETURN TO WORK

This right is subject to the same criteria as maternity pay. A woman not only has to inform her employer that she is leaving 21 days in advance, but also that she intends to come back to work. In the UK, a woman has up to 29 weeks after her baby is born in which she can return to work. Again, she has to give 21 days notice to her employer of her intention to return. Employers have the right to request a woman's intentions to return to work in writing.

These rights are generally available to all female employees, but they are all subject to conditions and limitations. All the rights except those relating to time off for antenatal care require a minimum period of employment. The statutory rights are minimum rights and do not affect the position where there are better provisions in an employee's contract. From 1994 pregnant women throughout the European Community will qualify for up to 14 weeks maternity leave, irrespective of their length of service. This follows the adoption of a new EC directive. Also, women's right to reinstatement or compensation for dismissal because of pregnancy will be maintained, but without the need for qualifying periods of service.

EXERCISE

Assuming a pregnant woman has worked full-time for an employer for six years and fulfilled all the legal requirements, make a list of all the rights she is entitled to. Also, make a list of as many ways as possible an employer might assist employees with childcare responsibilities.

PARENTAL LEAVE

In the UK, there is no statutory provision for paternity leave, parental leave, or leave to care for sick children. However, an increasing number of employers are including provision for paternity leave in their employee's terms and conditions, though in general through individual agreements rather than collective agreements. The usual amount of time off is three days, which can be taken any time around the birth of a child.

Several good employers have started to respond more seriously to the needs of female employees with children. A growing number of trade unions now include childcare issues in negotiations with employers. Many trade unions have pointed out that publicly funded childcare services and statutory employment rights are needed, and that relying on informal and haphazard arrangements is not enough.

Childcare issues have gained priority on the UK political and economic agendas as well as on the Brussels agenda. The Government's main response has been to encourage employers to introduce special schemes, such as career breaks, flexible hours, and job sharing. In 1992, a 12 member Working Group on Women's Issues appointed by the secretary of state for Employment, set the expansion of childcare services for working women as a major priority.

Although the Government has initiated these measures, the responsibility of putting them into practice has been left to employers and parents. In the UK, very little government funding has been pooled into this important issue. Much of the praise for any improvements hitherto implemented is due to the goodwill of the best employers. Companies which have introduced nursery provision include Mars, Midland bank, Thames Television, Sainsbury's, Rover, British Aerospace, and the BBC.

OTHER TYPES OF DISCRIMINATION

DISABILITY

In the USA, the 'Americans with Disabilities Act' was introduced in 1990 to provide anti-discrimination measures for the 43 million Americans with disabilities. In the UK, since 1983, ten anti-discrimination bills have been put forward to parliament to ban discrimination on the basis of disability and to provide disabled people with the same rights in education, employment and housing as able-bodied people. Unfortunately, none of the bills have been accepted and become law. In the UK, only 30 per cent of disabled people of working age have actually got jobs.

THE DISABLED PERSONS (EMPLOYMENT) ACTS 1944 AND 1958

These two laws still remain in force today. They introduced three main measures:

1 The setting up of a voluntary register of people with disabilities. The register of disabled persons (RDP) is kept by the Employment Service at local job centres. Registration is voluntary and is open to people with disabilities who already have jobs as well as those who are unemployed. Registration carries a number of benefits and certain job schemes are only available to those who register.

D ISCUSSION POINT

Many people with disabilities do not register, partly through fear that they may well be discriminated against even before they go along for a job interview. What do you think are the advantages and disadvantages of registering?

2 The introduction of the quota scheme. If an organisation employs 20 or more people, the law states that at least three per cent should be registered disabled people. An employer who fails to meet this quota is committing an offence if he or she engages anyone other than a registered disabled person, unless a permit has been obtained from the Department of Employment. In order to monitor whether suitable registered disabled persons are available and applying for jobs, the application form should ask whether the applicant is registered as disabled.

3 Reservation of vacancies in certain jobs for people with disabilities under the Designated Employment Scheme. Under this scheme entry into car park and lift attendant jobs has been reserved by the Secretary of State for registered disabled people.

THE CHRONICALLY SICK AND DISABLED PERSONS ACT 1970

Introduced in 1970 this law provides a legal framework for promoting the wellbeing of disabled people at community level. For the first time, it enabled local authorities to respond to the needs of the disabled in their areas rather than answer to a blanket approach from central government. The Act was updated in 1976 and stated that access, parking and sanitary facilities for disabled employees should be included in all new and newly converted premises where people work.

THE COMPANIES ACT 1985

Unlike the quota scheme which only applies to registered disabled people, the Companies Act applies to all employees with disabilities, registered or not. It applies to all companies which employ an average of 250 workers. Employers affected by this law must contain in their annual directors report a statement about their employment practices with regard to the following:

1 Measures which have been taken in the workplace to give full and equal consideration to workers with disabilities in recruitment. The policy adopted must focus on the abilities and aptitudes of workers, not on their disabilities.
2 Measures which have been taken in respect of workers who have been affected by a disability while working for the organisation. It is worth noting that 70 per cent of people who become disabled do so while at work. Therefore, the steps an employer takes to arrange training, or alternative work for the employee must be included in the report.
3 Steps the company has taken for the on-going career development and promotion of workers with disabilities, for example, special training schemes, equipment, outside assistance, and help with travel to and from the workplace.

THE DISABLED PERSONS ACT 1981

This Act introduced, for the first time, measures to enhance the mobility of people with disabilities. It stated that providers of premises should make special provision for access to buildings, and mobility within them. It recommends that all buildings conform to the standards laid down in the code of practice for access for the disabled in buildings. In practice, this might include building ramps for wheelchair access, widening doorways, wheelchair lifts, hoists or stairlifts.

EXERCISE

Think about the public buildings in your area: the library, swimming baths, courts and shopping centres. How many of them have got ramps for wheelchair access, ground floor toilets and lifts? What about the building you are sitting in at the moment – how does it compare?

CODE OF PRACTICE

In 1984, the Government's Employment Service published a code of good practice on the employment of disabled people. The code recommends that advertisements and application forms include a short statement welcoming applications from people with disabilities. It should be made clear on all forms that information supplied will be treated in complete confidence.

Copies of the code may be obtained from the Placing, Assessment and Counselling Team at local job centres or through a local Department of Employment office. Far more than laws, the code is a working document for organisations to adopt. The main sections of the code focus on:

• workers with disabilities as completely effective employees;
• the law on the employment of people with disabilities and the duties it places on employers;

- a practical step-by-step guide to recruiting workers with disabilities, which has total regard for the concerns employers may initially have;
- help for employees who become disabled;
- assistance with drawing up a policy and putting it into practice;
- sources of help and advice.

EXERCISE

Research either one of the Acts of Parliament discussed above or the code of practice on the employment of disabled people. Present a summary of its contents to your group. (Information about the Acts will be available from your local library, Department of Employment's Placing, Advisory and Counselling Team, or the welfare rights service.)

EMPLOYERS' AGENDA ON DISABILITY

In 1992, the Employers' Forum on Disability launched an Employers' Agenda on Disability, ten points for action to promote the recognition, recruitment and career development of people with disabilities. The agenda is backed by over 20 leading UK employers, including Barclays Bank Plc, Midland Bank Plc, Boots, The Post Office, British Rail and London Weekend Television, all of them members of the Forum. It also has the support of the Prime Minister. The member organisations have agreed to adopt the Agenda as their own, to share their experiences as they develop this fresh approach, and to call on others to follow their lead.

The ten points for action are:

1 *Equal opportunities policy and procedures statement*
The employment of people with disabilities will form an integral part of all equal opportunities policies and practices.
2 *Staff training and disability awareness*
The company will take specific steps to raise awareness of disability throughout the organisation, particularly targeting all staff involved in recruitment and selection processes.
3 *The working environment*
The company will take all reasonable steps to ensure that the working environment does not prevent disabled people from taking up positions for which they are suitably qualified.
4 *Recruitment*
The company will review and develop recruitment procedures which encourage applications from, and the employment of, people with disabilities.
5 *Career development*
The company will take specific steps to ensure that disabled people have the same opportunity as other staff to develop their full potential within the company.
6 *Retention, retraining and redevelopment*
Any employees who become disabled will be given the fullest support to return to a role appropriate to their experiences and ability within the company.

7 *Training and work experience*
   The company will ensure that disabled people are involved in work experience, training and education/industry links.

8 *People with disabilities in society*
   The company will respond to disabled people as customers, suppliers, shareholders, and members of the community at large.

9 *The full involvement of disabled people*
   When implementing the ten points for action, the company will encourage the participation of disabled employees to ensure that, wherever possible, employment practices recognise and meet their needs.

10 *Monitoring performance*
   The company will monitor its progress in implementing the key points. There will be an annual audit of performance reviewed at board level. Achievements and objectives will be published to employees and in the UK annual report.

AIDS AND HIV

A new Charter banning discrimination against employees with AIDS or the HIV virus was launched in June 1992 by the charity *National Aids Trust*, with the support of 16 top British companies. Founder members included The Body Shop, Marks and Spencer, Midland Bank Plc, Sainsbury's, IBM, and Levi Strauss (UK) Ltd. These companies have signed up to the 'Companies act! Business Charter', pledging themselves to the principle of non discrimination when dealing with employees or potential employees who have AIDS or who are HIV positive. Some of the Charter's supporters already have their own anti-discrimination policies in place, while others are in the process of preparing them. The impetus for the Charter has come from cases brought to the attention of the Trust where people with AIDS or HIV have lost their jobs either through direct or indirect discrimination by their employers. The Charter has the support of the government. More information about the Charter and how an organisation can become involved is available from the *National Aids Trust*.

DISCUSSION POINT

In general, what are the risks of becoming HIV positive through normal workplace practice? Make a list of jobs which you consider there might be a higher than average risk.

EX-OFFENDERS

Over five million people in Britain have a criminal record and ex-offenders are more likely to experience unemployment than non-offenders. This is not only a waste of human resources, but in the 1990s when skill shortages are becoming more widespread, employers need to consider recruiting from as wide a pool of potential employees as possible. In the long term, the discrimination which many ex-offenders face when applying for a job is to the disadvantage of the employer and employee alike.

D ISCUSSION POINT

> Imagine you are an employer about to launch an annual recruitment campaign. Make a list of the concerns you might have if you were considering employing a person with a record of past offences. Can these concerns really be justified or should you, as a forward thinking employer, concentrate on the present and future rather than on the past?

THE REHABILITATION OF OFFENDERS ACT 1974

This law is the specific legislation affecting ex-offenders' job opportunities. In practice it enables ex-offenders to wipe the slate clean of their criminal record provided that they are not convicted of another offence during a specified period of time. At the end of that time the offence is then said to have become 'spent' (in practice, ignored or forgotten). The length of time required for an ex-offender to become rehabilitated depends on the sentence received for the conviction. Each sentence carries its own rehabilitation period. Custodial sentences for over two and a half years in length can never become spent. The main advantage of the system is that if ex-offenders are asked on a job application form if they have a criminal record, it need not be revealed at all if they so wish. It is illegal for an employer to discriminate against an ex-offender on the grounds of his or her spent conviction. However, there are a number of exceptions to this, some of them are outlined below:

- work involving matters of national security, for example, some posts in the civil service;
- work which is mainly concerned with vulnerable groups, for instance, the elderly, mentally ill, children and young people.

For these jobs, the law states that ex-offenders must declare any conviction, caution or bind over, even if they would otherwise be regarded as spent under the Act.

THE NATIONAL ASSOCIATION FOR THE CARE AND RESETTLEMENT OF OFFENDERS (NACRO)

NACRO is a voluntary organisation that advises on all educational and training matters for ex-offenders in the UK. It also runs a number of training projects and Youth Training programmes, and their training centres can advise employers and ex-offenders about services which are available locally.

THE APEX TRUST

The Apex Trust is a national network agency working to improve the employment prospects of ex-offenders. It operates 30 training centres which run a range of courses matched to the local labour market needs. It also runs job clubs throughout the country which provide training in job search skills and interview techniques, and runs a job placement and advice service for ex-offenders. The Trust has produced a guide on good practice for the employment of people with criminal records which has been approved by the Institute of Personnel Management. The guide is called *Releasing the Potential* and is available through the Trust. It brings together good policy and practice in the field of employment of ex-offenders.

EXERCISE

Find out about the range of services which are offered by NACRO and the Apex Trust in your area. The addresses can be obtained through telephone directories or directory enquiries.

AGE

The number of older people in society is increasing. While this in itself is excellent evidence of the medical advances in promoting good health and disease control, it does bring with it its own set of problems. For example, older people do not form a single group with identical needs and circumstances. They may be either workers or retired. Also, of course, they may be black or white, disabled or able-bodied and male or female.

In spite of the growing number of older people, there is no specific law to protect their rights. In the European Community, France is the only member state with laws prohibiting age discrimination. In the USA, a law called the Age Discrimination in Employment Act was introduced in 1967 to protect older workers from discrimination on the grounds of age. Age discrimination occurs in many ways: in recruitment by placing upper age limits on jobs, and in promotion and training by overlooking older workers, solely on the grounds of age. A 1989 survey by the company MSL showed that of 1,284 executive or management posts advertised, over 85 per cent had an upper age limit of 40.

EXERCISE

Subtle forms of age discrimination can still be found in job advertisements which don't necessarily include upper age limits. Statements such as 'Young energetic person required' or, 'Aged between 25 and 40, the ideal candidate will . . .' are just as ageist as those which actually impose upper age limits. Scan the situations vacant columns of local and national newspapers; how widespread is this practice?

EMPLOYMENT (AGE LIMITS) BILL

Treating an older person less favourably than a younger person is unacceptable in whatever form it takes. The Government believes that employers should not impose upper age limits and they are urging employers to make greater use of the skills, experience and expertise of older people. In 1989, a bill was passed to end workplace discrimination of older people. It was called the Employment (age limits) Bill, but was unfortunately too late for the House of Commons at that session. No further progress on the bill has occurred to date.

SEXUALITY OR SEX ORIENTATION

Specific laws aimed at protecting the rights of gays and lesbians are uncommon, although an increasing number of organisations are now including sex orientation in their equal opportunities policies and 'welcoming applications' from these groups in their job advertisements. However, in spite of small areas of progress at company level, this has not been matched by any effort on the part of central government to address the issue of equal opportunities for gays and lesbians. Work began in 1990 on a Homosexual Equality Bill in order for discrimination on the grounds of homosexuality be treated as a disciplinary matter. However, the bill's sponsors, namely the Stonewall Group, the Campaign for Homosexual Equality and the National Council for Civil Liberties have received very little support from policy makers.

EUROPEAN COMMUNITY MEASURES

The EC has introduced laws and action programmes to promote equal opportunities. Within the field of equality, its measures focus on sex discrimination, age and disability. Little has been achieved in promoting equality and non-discrimination on the grounds of race and sexuality. To date the European Commission has adopted five Directives on equality of opportunity for men and women. Community law on equal treatment between men and women consists of Article 119 of the Treaty of Rome which states that men and women should receive equal pay for equal work, and five equality Directives. Directives have the force of law; the EC decides what must happen but leaves it to member states to introduce national laws to comply with the Directive.

The five Directives are:

1 The equal pay Directive
2 Directive on equal treatment in employment, which has banned all sex based discrimination at work
3 The social security Directive which is aimed at achieving equal treatment for women and men in social security schemes
4 The fourth Directive on occupational social security schemes extends the rule of equal treatment in social security to include occupational social security schemes
5 The self-employed Directive relates to the provision of equal treatment for women who are self employed, or who work entirely or partly with their spouses

At the end of 1991 the European Commission agreed to adopt a Directive on pregnancy at work. From 1994 pregnant women throughout the European Community will qualify for up to 14 weeks of maternity leave irrespective of their length of service with their employer

DISCUSSION POINT

In general, it is believed that in light of the single European market an increasing amount of law in future will be generated in Brussels rather than in national parliaments. What are the advantages and disadvantages of this for employees and employers? For example, one advantage could be that at least the law will be consistent and employees in Lisbon, for instance, will have similar rights as those in Madrid or Luxemburg. However, can laws which are formed in Brussels really respond to differences in local needs in Liverpool and Florence, for example?

THE EUROPEAN COMMISSION'S ACTION PROGRAMMES

EQUAL OPPORTUNITIES FOR WOMEN 1991–1995

This action programme is the third of its kind and lays down three main courses of action:

1 To apply the legal framework under the equality directives so that equal opportunities for women becomes a fact rather than just a legal right on paper.
2 To promote the integration of women into all sectors of paid employment.
3 To improve the status of women in society.

DISABILITY

The HELIOS programme is to run 1992–1996. It stands for Handicapped People Living Independently in an Open Society. The programme's aims include:

- on-going development of vocational training centres;
- financial help towards the cost of adapting premises to accommodate handicapped people, for instance, by constructing ramps for wheelchair access, lifts, hoists, ground-floor toilets and kitchen facilities;
- start-up assistance for schemes designed to increase the number of people with disabilities in useful employment. In practice, this can include a whole range of special aids and equipment, such as personal reader services for employees with visual handicaps.

OLDER PEOPLE

In 1991, an EC action programme for older people was launched. The launch focussed on a range of subjects including the social integration of older people, and their right to independent living. The Commission has agreed to set up an information system on European-wide organisations and schemes which are concerned with the needs of older people. This will help in the exchange of ideas and good practice between member states. Also, 1993 has been nominated as the European Year of the Elderly and measures to assist older people in a whole range of ways have been developed right throughout the Community. Information on all of the equality programmes within the EC can be obtained from the European Commission or from Age Concern.

FURTHER READING

Collins, H. *Equality matters: equal opportunities in the 90s: background and current issues* The Library Association, 1992

Collins, H. *Equal opportunities handbook: a comprehensive guide to law and best practice in Europe* Blackwell, 1992

Morris, J. *Pride against prejudice: transforming attitudes to disability* The Women's Press, 1991

Straw, J. *Equal opportunities, the way ahead* Institute of Personnel Management, 1989

THE EMPLOYMENT CONTRACT AND TERMS AND CONDITIONS OF EMPLOYMENT

Employee relations are about the interaction between employers and the people who work for them, or their representatives. In large organisations, employees are often represented by trade unions or staff associations. The wider definition of employee relations includes relationships at a national level between all those involved in negotiating working conditions for employees, and those involved in making sure that employers get the best out of their workforce. For example, national decisions made on minimum wage levels in a given industry affect every single member of that industry group from Cornwall to Newcastle.

The majority of organisations aim to provide a good working relationship between managers and employees. This is simply common sense, both in economic and human terms: legal disputes are expensive, time consuming, and in the end counter productive to good working relationships.

Behind even the smallest transaction there is an enormous body of legislation which those involved can refer to if they disagree over an issue. These laws have increased in volume and complexity over the last few decades, and with the increasing volume of goods and services generated by the single European market are likely to become even more complex.

WHAT IS A CONTRACT?

A contract is a legally binding document. Basic guidelines to the English laws of contract state that the following rules must be observed:

1 That there must be an offer and acceptance of agreement, which must be of a lawful nature.
2 Consideration (i.e. some form of payment or other remuneration, for example, exchange of payment for labour) must be provided.
3 The legal status of either party may affect the validity of a contract (for instance a sale of an unlawful item or service to a person under the age of 18, or in some

cases 16, can be set aside in certain circumstances, therefore making the contract invalid).

It should be remembered that a contract does not have to be in writing, but in the context of employment it makes it easier to prove that an agreement exists if it is written down. It is worth noting how often in fact people make contracts without consciously realising it: buying goods in a supermarket, boarding a taxi or train, or buying clothes from a catalogue. In general, it is only when things go wrong that people start to question just what their legal rights are.

EXERCISE

Collect a range of contracts which group members have received for buying goods or services in the past. It might be for a new stereo or aeroplane tickets from a travel agent, for example. What rights and obligations does the contract place on the seller and on the buyer? How easy do you feel it would be to obtain compensation in the event of something going wrong?

In the UK there are several consumer groups which exist to help customers solve disputes over faulty goods, poor services, or poor products. Try to find out which groups can be contacted for advice in your area.

THE EMPLOYMENT CONTRACT

Before an individual joins an organisation, their contract of employment has been through a number of stages which have involved different groups of people at different times. Most contracts are the end result of a series of processes between a range of people representing different clients. The usual channels through which contracts are drawn up include:

- managers or owners;
- the shop steward: a person elected by the workforce whose main job is to convey the views of the workers to management;
- the works committee: there is an increasing trend in employee relations towards greater staff involvement and participation in the overall running of an organisation. The works committee – on which both workers and managers have representatives – is a major step forward towards improving such communication;
- a consultative committee: a similar group to a works committee but tends to be found only in very large organisations where a wide range of issues needs to be addressed and reviewed regularly.

The employment contract is the main document which contains details about the terms and conditions of employment. Even with the tendency in the last few decades towards increased participation by everyone in the day-to-day running of an organisation, it is still the case in practice that the majority of employees have very little say in their contracts of employment. More typically, depending on the size of a business, agreements on wage rates, hours of work, the type of work undertaken, bonus schemes and holidays are drawn up by negotiation between employers and their employees' representatives. The individual agrees merely to join the organisation on the pre-designed terms and conditions.

EXERCISE

> If an organisation does not provide a single document outlining the terms and conditions of employment, what written documents could include these details? Think of your own work if you are in employment; what is written down about your job? Where can you find documents which contain this information?

WHO IS LEGALLY ENTITLED TO A WRITTEN STATEMENT?

It is good practice to give every employee a written contract which sets out all the details about the job, such as pay and overtime rates, holiday pay, hours of work and what the job entails. If these things are not in writing there may be arguments later about what contractual terms were agreed, which could be costly and time consuming. Under the Employment Protection (Consolidation) Act 1978, most workers have a right to a 'written statement of their terms and conditions of employment'. The law as to which groups are legally entitled to a written statement is that:

- employees who work 16 hours or more a week must be given a written statement within 13 weeks of starting work;
- employees who work less than 16 hours but more than 8 hours a week have the right to a written statement after five years with an employer;
- employees who work less than 8 hours a week do not have the right to a written statement.

All new employees have a right to receive a formal letter of acceptance from their new employer confirming their appointment. Even if employees are not entitled to a written statement by law, it is good practice to issue each employee with one. An employee's contract cannot be changed without his or her agreement. A formal letter of acceptance should contain the following details:

- a firm offer of work;
- hours of work;
- the standard office opening and closing hours;
- the start date and time, and the name of the person the new employee should report to.

Essentially, the relationship between the individual employee and his or her employer is formally structured by the contract of employment. Employee relations however, are about human relations, and interests, shared hobbies, and friendships often develop, which are not subject to a formal structure or piece of documentation. It should be remembered though, that the contractual details constitute an important formal agreement upon which the future relationship is to be based. Like all contracts, there are three major components to an employee's contract, which in order of priority are:

1 The minimum legal requirements or statutory rights
2 Expressed terms
3 Implied terms

THE MINIMUM LEGAL REQUIREMENTS

When someone becomes an employee they automatically become eligible to rights under the law. These include rights to equal pay, the right to belong to a trade union and the right not to be discriminated against on the grounds of race or sex.

Employees also have the right to keep their jobs, on the same conditions, when a firm changes hands, for example, in the event of a merger or take-over occurring. There are also other rights which some workers may have, depending on how long they have worked for the same employer, and on how many hours they work. These include:

- The right to a payslip
- The right to a certain period of notice
- The right to written reasons for dismissal
- The right to redundancy pay
- The right not to be unfairly dismissed

The minimum legal requirements in the UK are, in fact, very limited, with the exception of a few occupations. In practice, most people agree to contracts which in effect state that they can work for as long as they want, for as little money as they like. There are few limitations in law, with the exceptions of airline pilots, cabin crews and HGV drivers, where the number of hours of work at any one session are restricted by law.

The main legal requirements in most jobs centre on:

- written information which has to be supplied between the employer and the employee;
- periods of notice for terminations of a contract (at least a week's notice should always be given);
- safety: minimum requirements and procedures for compliance with health and safety laws.

Employees are also entitled to guaranteed payments when their company cannot provide them with work on a given day or week, to statutory sick pay, and in a few particular industries, to a minimum wage. The guarantee payments limit on a days pay during short-time or temporary lay off in 1992 was £14.10. The statutory sick pay limit for earnings between £54 to £190 per week was £45.30, and for earnings over £190 per week, £52.50. Minimum wages are determined by an industry's wage council, though not all industries are covered by them. A wage council is a meeting between employers, unions and an independent body appointed by the Government to set up minimum wages for an industry. Industries which are not covered by wage councils have, in practice, no obligations to provide a minimum wage and can therefore pay whatever they like.

D ISCUSSION POINT

What are the advantages to employees working in industries where minimum wages are governed by a wages council? Should all industries be similarly covered?

THE EXPRESSED TERMS

The expressed terms are any written details of agreements between an individual and an employing organisation. If a legal requirement and expressed term are at odds, then the legal requirement takes precedence.

A contract comes into operation the moment an employee starts work. Even if there is no written evidence in the form of a formal document, the courts and industrial tribunals are able, by law, to 'infer' or surmise contractual details from the behaviour of the two parties. In practice, this means that if an employer provides work and pay and an individual continues to work and receive his or her pay, then both parties are deemed to be under a contract of employment. It should be noted, however, that a written contract is much to the advantage of both parties, since details can be more accurately inferred from written rather than verbal agreements.

The range of expressed terms is enormous. Some organisations provide staff with no written details, and prefer instead to direct the employee to company handbooks or other details which include the rules of the company. These may include:

- Union handbooks
- Work rule books
- Job descriptions and personnel specifications
- Departmental notices and guidelines

Also, as previously mentioned, there is now a requirement upon employers to provide their employees with a written statement of the main terms and conditions of employment before 13 weeks in the post have expired. In most cases this means a contract of employment.

The written contract can include any details, but must contain the following:

- the names of both parties to the contract (that is, the employer and the employee);
- start date of employment, and whether any previous employment is to count towards working out years of continuous employment (for instance, for the purposes of pensions, maternity leave or maternity rights);
- job title (a job description is not absolutely necessary but still very helpful);
- wages or salary and any other form of remuneration, how they are calculated, and the intervals at which they are paid (weekly or monthly);
- hours of work and normal working hours;
- holiday entitlement, holiday pay and public holidays;

- conditions relating to pensions;
- conditions relating to sickness, injuries (sustained in or out of work) and sick pay;
- length of notice the employee is obliged to give and entitled to receive. As far as the employee is concerned, he or she is bound to give a certain length of notice when intending to leave the job. This may exceed the statutory minimum but cannot be less. The length of the minimum period of notice depends on how long an individual has worked for an employer, varying from one week to a month or, in some cases, as long as six months;
- grievance and disciplinary procedures, including the name of the person an employee should contact if dissatisfied with disciplinary proceedings or with the result of a disciplinary decision.

HOURS OF WORK

There is little statutory regulation of hours of work in the UK. Some groups of workers (for example, HGV drivers, airline pilots and cabin crew) have maximum limits on their working hours, but for most workers, hours of work are set by their contracts of employment. Employers should make clear what the basic contractual hours are, and the days on which they will be worked, for example, 37 hours between Monday and Friday. Hours are normally expressed as a weekly total. However, in companies working shift systems, hours are sometimes calculated on an annual basis. In some cases it may be appropriate to state how many hours must be worked on each day of the week.

E X E R C I S E

Talk to someone you know who works shifts. How are his or her hours of work divided and calculated? Does the employee have much say or flexibility in determining his or her hours of work? How does the pay rate differ for night shifts and weekend working? Present a summary of your findings to your group.

Whatever the contractual hours, it is important to ensure that there is a clearly understood system of recording attendance. This will avoid disputes arising later on, especially where pay systems are closely linked to actual hours worked in each pay period. Basic working hours in Britain and the rest of Europe have been slowly reduced over the past two decades.

In June 1990 the European Commission proposed a Working Time Directive which contained proposals to limit the length of the working week across the EC to a maximum of 48 hours. The Directive lays down minimum holidays and rest breaks, which many British Government Ministers feel would impose enormous costs on many employers. Denmark and Ireland, like Britain, have very few restrictions on working hours, and generally leave it to employers and staff to decide the matter themselves. In the UK some 2.5 million employees including many construction and postal workers, security guards, hotel and catering staff, agricultural workers and maintenance staff, regularly work overtime which takes them beyond the proposed 48 hour limit. The Working Time Directive has been put forward under the health and safety provisions of the Treaty of Rome. Listed below is a summary of its proposals:

- maximum working week across the Community to be 48 hours, including overtime, averaged out over a period of three months;
- all workers entitled to a minimum of four weeks paid holiday each year;
- minimum daily rest period of 11 hours, weekly break of 35 hours;
- certain restrictions on night work.

FLEXIBLE WORKING HOURS

Some employers recognise the need for their employees to be given greater flexibility over how and when they work their contracted hours. Flexible working time (FWT) is a system which is used to give more control to employees, usually over their starting and finishing time. Generally speaking, it allows for workers to be at the job within a specific core time, usually between 10 a.m. and midday and between 2 p.m. and 4 p.m. Outside the core hours, employees may arrange their time to suit themselves, provided that they work the contracted weekly hours over an accounting period, usually four weeks. FWT may not suit small organisations or those where continuous cover is required. It may cost more in terms of overheads such as heating and lighting if the workplace is open longer each day for individual workers to arrive early or stay late outside the core time. On the other hand, FWT is seen as a useful perk to many employees and to job seekers. For organisations considering introducing FWT it is important that the workforce is consulted beforehand and agreements reached in advance on whether the system is to be compulsory or voluntary, and what are to be the means of recording times. There are two main methods of recording hours worked in organisations which provide FWT:

- clocking in;
- completing flexitime sheets at the end of each day, and handing them over to a departmental supervisor at the end of each week.

D ISCUSSION POINT

Write a list of industries and jobs you think are ideally suited to FWT, and those for which you consider that it would not be practical. What are the advantages of FWT for employees?

THE IMPLIED TERMS

As well as statutory rights, and rights which are written into the contract, employees and employers have other rights which are assumed to be a part of the contract. These are referred to as the implied terms. They include issues such as 'acting in good faith towards each other' and 'taking care to ensure health and safety in the workplace'. Implied terms are the third component of employment contracts, and are less easy to define than expressed terms and minimum legal requirements. To understand the meaning of these terms, think about this situation: an airline pilot based at Heathrow Airport is asked to sweep the floor and clean out the public toilets instead of his or her normal duties involved in flying aircraft.

Even if there was no written statement of the terms and conditions of employment the pilot could refuse, since arguably it is not part of a pilot's job to sweep floors or clean out toilets. Of course, most cases are less clear than this, but in almost every contract the range of options is limited by realistic expectations of what the actual job implies.

Even if an employer does not write certain terms into a contract, an industrial tribunal may decide that they are 'implied terms' simply because they are custom and practice in a firm. This may include issues such as the right to paid bank holidays, or less obvious things like the right to buy goods manufactured by your firm at a discount.

EXERCISE

Research an employment contract belonging to an employee working for a large organisation. Write a summary of its major features under the following headings for distribution among your group:

- The minimum legal terms
- The expressed terms
- The implied terms (you may have to discuss these with the employee since they are often not formally written into a contract)

CHANGES TO AN EMPLOYMENT CONTRACT

In theory, the terms and conditions of the contract must be made in writing. If there is a change of employer, such as in a take-over bid, all employees must be notified of their employer's new name and the date on which their continuous employment begins.

Changes are made to the contract of employment by agreement between the two parties, generally through management and union agreement. In practice, many changes are introduced without any direct formal agreement with employees or their representatives. Sometimes, employers may introduce changes and rely on the goodwill of their staff to comply with them. Problems arise when changes are made to the contract without clear notification or agreement. Serious difficulties may arise, for instance, when the location at which employees work is changed or when procedures relating to injuries at work are altered without due notification. Clarity is also a problem where changes to the implied terms occur, which by their nature are subject to different interpretations. In general, it is important to remember three things:

- if an employer wishes to change terms and conditions of employment, these changes must be negotiated with employees or their representatives. If an employer changes an employee's terms and conditions without agreement, he or she is likely to be in breach of contract. This is true whether there is a written statement or not. So, if a manager changes an employee's terms and conditions of employment without negotiation, he may face legal action by the employee concerned;

- if changes in the written statement have been agreed between the employee and employer, the employer must provide written evidence of the changes. These should be given to the employee as soon as possible, but no later than one month after the changes have occurred;

- if a full written statement outlining the changes has not been issued, but an employer has indicated that the relevant details can be found elsewhere, then these details must be brought up to date within a month.

DIFFERENT TYPES OF CONTRACT

In general, there are three types of employment contract:

1 Permanent contracts
2 Temporary contracts
3 Sub-contracts

PERMANENT CONTRACTS

These are contracts whereby the employer and employee agree to a continuous employment relationship. As such, permanent contracts have no termination date. They may continue until either party issues the other with a 'notice' to end the agreement. In the case of the employee, this is usually a length of time he or she gives to the employer that he or she is considering leaving the organisation. In the case of the employer, it may be a redundancy notice.

TEMPORARY CONTRACTS

In recent years, several organisations have grown away from the notion of permanent contracts and have started to issue only temporary contracts. Temporary contracts include a starting date and a finishing date in their guidelines. It may be for a matter of months or years, though twelve months is a more common period. Vacancies arising out of maternity leave absences are very often based on temporary contracts of five to six months to cover the original postholder's maternity leave period. Seasonal jobs, such as hotel employment and seaside work are also generally subject to temporary contracts. Individuals with a temporary contract of employment should ensure that they have equal rights and conditions under the contract as their peers on permanent contracts.

EXERCISE

Survey the periodicals, journals and newspapers on display in your local library. In the jobs pages, list those vacancies which are advertising a temporary or 'fixed term' position. Approximately what percentage of advertisements are for temporary jobs and what percentage are for permanent jobs? What are the advantages and disadvantages of temporary contracts from both the employer's and employee's angle?

SUBCONTRACTS

These are issued by organisations when they need to bring in specialist skills for a specified time period. For example, an office block may need decorating and the work may be subcontracted to a painting and decorating company. Or a computer software company may need specialist programmers to work on a specialist project. If the company has not already got the necessary skills, it might subcontract the project, or part of it, to another organisation or individual who has those specialist skills.

EMPLOYEE RIGHTS UNDER THE LAW

In summary, employment legislation and contracts of employment provide rights for both employees and employers. Broadly, the laws governing employment have set up a number of 'protections' to cover each stage of working life, including:

* Recruitment
* Remuneration (salary, wages and bonuses)
* Redundancy or dismissal
* Retirement

And not forgetting all the periods in between recruitment and retirement, such as sick-leave, maternity or paternity leave, holiday entitlement and special incentive schemes or perks. The rights these laws give employers and employees are outlined below:

* the right not to be discriminated against in recruitment or employment on the grounds of race or marital status;
* the right to a written statement (before the first 13 weeks in employment have expired) covering the main terms and conditions of employment;
* the right to work in safe working conditions which comply at least to national minimum standards;
* the right not to be discriminated against on the grounds of trade union membership and union activities;
* the right to full payment as agreed;
* in the case of women, the right not to be dismissed for reasons of pregnancy, and to have time off for antenatal care (for more information on maternity rights see Chapter 4);
* the right to return to work following illness;
* the right not to be unfairly dismissed;
* the right to a written explanation if dismissed;
* on being made redundant any employee with two years continuous service has the right to a lump sum of money. The amount payable varies, depending on length of service, age and weekly pay. Employers are required to consult appropriate trade unions about proposed redundancies and to disclose reasonably full details to unions and employees in writing of their intentions. This information should include:
  – reasons for the redundancies;

- number of employees who will be affected;
- a description of employees (for example, office workers, machine operators, supervisors etc.);
- method of selection;
- how and when the method of implementing the redundancies is going to happen.

THE ADVISORY CONCILIATION AND ARBITRATION SERVICE (ACAS)

One of the functions of an employee relations specialist is to find out which services are provided by the government. After all, the government sets the legal and economic framework in place, so it is crucial to understand the influence the government has on day-to-day industrial relations. ACAS is one such service which has a direct role to play in employee relations by intervening in situations which have become difficult.

ACAS helps sort out some of the industrial relations problems faced by unions, employees and employers. It was set up in the 1970s to act as a third party in industrial disputes. ACAS have authority to issue codes of practice, which although not legally binding, may be used as evidence in court. The ACAS codes are short and practical outlines which operate in much the same way as the highway code, for example. Although it is not unlawful to ignore the highway code, the police can still argue in court that a driver's failure to follow the code is convincing evidence of an offence. The ACAS code operates in a similar way.

ACAS is directed by a council which includes members drawn from both the employers and trade union sides of industry. ACAS does not charge for its services – any employer, trade union or employee can approach ACAS for information or advice on industrial relations matters. This may, for example, relate to some aspect of employment law such as the maternity rights of only one woman. On the other hand, it may be about an employee relations issue which is affecting the entire workforce. ACAS may have to conduct a survey of the organisation in order to assess the situation, or occasionally a series of short visits may be undertaken to advise the company on how to handle matters.

In its main role as a third party organisation, ACAS is involved in:

1 advice: giving advice to employers and employees;
2 conciliation: a process under which an independent outsider acts as a new line of communication between employers and employees. The conciliator will usually try to meet both parties separately at first, in order to make an independent assessment of both parties' cases. Afterwards, he or she may attempt to bring them together to continue the talks;
3 arbitration: this involves both parties agreeing to accept the recommendations of an independent body such as ACAS;
4 mediation: this is a weightier process than conciliation, whereby a mediator

proposes the basis for a settlement between the two parties. However, the proposal does not have to be accepted.

Who is entitled to use ACAS? Do you think an external group or third party organisation such as ACAS is a necessary component of industrial relations? List as many benefits as you can think of which may be derived from a third party opinion in employment disputes.

DISMISSAL

Most cases of termination of employment are straightforward, and usually have more to do with an individual having found employment elsewhere than arising out of any problem. In a small minority of cases however, problems can arise over the dismissal of an employee. The purpose of the unfair dismissal provisions in the Employment Protection Act 1978, as amended by the Employment Act 1989, is to protect employees against any hardship resulting from being dismissed unfairly.

Although it is 20 years since the laws on unfair dismissal first came on to the statute book, it can still cause enormous problems to employers. One unfair dismissal can cost a company in excess of £20,000. The most common causes of unfair dismissal are ill health, absenteeism, general misconduct (whether genuine or suspected) and employees failing to carry out their duties satisfactorily. In the UK alone over 20,000 applications for unfair dismissal are filed each year. Of these, approximately one third are withdrawn early on in the procedure as being unlikely to succeed.

THE ACAS CODE OF PRACTICE ON DISCIPLINARY PRACTICE AND PROCEDURES

This document provides employers with practical advice on how to deal with disciplinary matters fairly, and aims to help employers to set up fair procedures for dealing with the type of problem which may lead to dismissal. Industrial tribunals take into account any provision of the code which appears to them to be relevant to any case before them. ACAS do not expect all employers to follow the code to the letter, but to decide to what extent it is practicable for an employer to do so given the size and resources of his or her firm.

The code makes it clear that management is responsible for maintaining discipline within the organisation and for ensuring that there are adequate disciplinary rules and procedures. To be fully effective, the rules and procedures need to be accepted as reasonable to those who are to be covered by them. It is important that management aims to secure the involvement of employees and all levels of management when making new rules or revising existing ones.

UNFAIR DISMISSAL

It should be noted that not everyone can claim unfair dismissal. The law excludes three main groups of people as well as several small exceptions from this protection. The three main groups are:

1 Employees past normal retirement age for their employment or, if there is no normal retirement age, have reached age 65. This means that an individual over the standard company retirement age can be dismissed without any legal penalty for the employer. Whatever their age, however, employees may complain to an industrial tribunal of unfair dismissal on account of trade union membership or activities or because they are not members of a trade union.
2 Part-time workers; in general, those who work less than 16 hours per week.
3 Employees with insufficient service: the law states that to claim unfair dismissal an individual must have worked for an organisation for a minimum of two years. This qualifying period does not apply at all for employees who have been dismissed on account of their trade union membership, or because they are not members of a trade union and have been dismissed because of it.

So what about those who can claim unfair dismissal? Obviously what constitutes unfair dismissal is open to quite subjective interpretation. In general, common sense should dictate how employees ought to behave in the workplace and in turn how managers ought to treat their employees. A manager has to be convinced that the reason for dismissal is a fair one. In practice, this means that a dismissal has to be due to:

• An employee's misconduct
• A lack of capability or aptitude to do his or her job properly
• Redundancy

By far the vast majority of cases fall under one of these three headings. Even if an employer is sure that the dismissal is fair, there is a further requirement which states that the dismissal must be reasonable and take the individual's circumstances into account.

DISCUSSION POINT

Take the simple case of stealing. If you were a manager would you dismiss an individual if what had been stolen was:

• A biro and two notebooks?
• A pair of scissors and a metal ruler?
• A stapler and a hole puncher?
• An old wordprocessor?
• Petty cash of £250?
• A company vehicle?

Obviously it would depend on the circumstances. Most people would not dismiss someone for stealing a biro, and an industrial tribunal would definitely find such a dismissal unfair. However, a company car or a large amount of company cash is a much more serious matter. Sometimes, exceptional cases arise where an employee may be having problems not related to his or her job, but which are having an adverse affect upon his or her normal workplace behaviour. In this instance, an employee may well require counselling or temporary supervision until the problems are sorted out. It is up to managers to view the situation as broadly as possible, and not merely treat an isolated offence as reason for dismissal. In the case of misconduct and lack of capability, tribunals will consider the circumstances under which a dismissal can be claimed as fair or unfair.

For misconduct cases, a tribunal expects that:

- employers (managers) will have given employees full instructions and warnings of the likely consequences of breaches of company rules;
- the individual concerned has had an opportunity to explain the reason for their behaviour before any decision to dismiss is taken. If the employee wishes, he or she ought to be allowed to be accompanied to any such hearing by a colleague or representative;
- any action taken in respect of misconduct goes through the proper disciplinary channels with a right of appeal to higher management if necessary.

In cases of lack of capability there are, in fact, two quite different forms. First, either the employee is very ill and as a consequence is off work for a long period, or is suitably fit but simply cannot carry out his or her job properly. In the first case, of long absences from work due to poor health, industrial tribunals are not keen to see employees dismissed but will accept it if:

- the demands of the company are such that the post must be filled;
- the employee's chances of full recovery and future prospects have been thoroughly covered, with the individual concerned present at any meeting whenever possible;
- the manager has considered alternatives (reduced hours, different work, home working etc);
- the individual has had sufficient warning of the possibility of dismissal.

In the case of lack of skill or poor performance where a person is incapable of carrying out the job properly, industrial tribunals expect the following:

- evidence that the employee really cannot do the job;
- evidence that the individual has had adequate help from management wherever possible, such as one-to-one coaching or special supervision, as well as a full explanation of the job description and what his or her main duties are;
- clear warnings that continued poor performance may lead to dismissal;
- that an employee has had an opportunity to explain why his or her performance is poor: it may be that the machines are faulty, or working conditions inadequate, or another valid reason which could explain why an employee is not able to carry out the job properly;
- that he or she has had an opportunity to appeal against the decision. This is important in order to safeguard against the fact that it might possibly be just one manager who is against the employee and wishes to see him or her dismissed.

REMEDIES FOR UNFAIR DISMISSAL

Employees have the right not to be unfairly dismissed, and those that think they have may seek a remedy by complaining to an industrial tribunal. A complaint must be received by the tribunal within three months of the date the job was terminated (this is usually the date of leaving the job). So if an employee leaves on 1 March, the industrial tribunal must be informed by 31 May at the latest. If a tribunal decides that a dismissal was indeed unfair there are three possible solutions it can propose:

- reinstatement in the job;
- re-engagement: this happens when an employee is re-employed but not necessarily in the same job or on the same terms and conditions of employment;
- compensation: this consists of a basic award which is calculated in the same way as a redundancy payment and, in addition, a compensatory award based on the employee's loss of earnings. In 1992, the maximum basic award limit on a week's pay was £5,940, and the maximum compensatory award was £10,000. The amounts increase approximately every 12 months.

REDUNDANCY

This is a painful situation for both employers and employees, since from a business point of view it is the ultimate sign of failure. Redundancy is the dismissal of all or part of the workforce; something which happens when an organisation closes down or cuts back on staff because of a fall in demand for its products. An employee who is made redundant in those circumstances cannot complain of unfair dismissal, but might be entitled to receive a tax-free lump sum under the State Redundancy Payments Scheme.

Employees who are made redundant have two main rights:

1 The right to a redundancy payment
2 The right to time off to look for other work

REDUNDANCY PAYMENTS

Under the Employment Protection (Consolidation) Act 1978 an employer must pay redundancy payments to employees who have been continuously employed for a certain period and who have been made redundant. The amount of payment depends on four factors: the employee's age, how many hours he or she work each week, how long they have worked for the company and their weekly salary.

AGE
- Employees aged under 18 are not entitled to redundancy payment;
- employees aged 65 and over are not entitled to redundancy payment;
- employees aged between 18 and 64 are entitled to:
  - half a week's pay for each complete year over the age of 18 and under the age of 22

– one week's pay for each complete year aged 22 or more but less than 41
– one and a half week's pay for each complete year aged 41 or more.

HOURS OF WORK

- Employees who work less than 8 hours a week have no rights to a redundancy payment;
- employees who work between 8 and 16 hours a week have no rights to a redundancy payment until they have worked for five years;
- employees who work 16 hours a week have rights to a redundancy payment after they have worked for the same employer for two years.

LENGTH OF SERVICE

Redundancy payments are calculated on the number of years continuous service an employee has had with the same employer from the age of 18 until the date the notice takes effect. Continuous service includes service in a business which has been taken over or merged with another. The maximum number of years service which can count to redundancy payment is 20.

WEEKLY EARNINGS

Redundancy payments are calculated on the basis of a week's pay. A week's pay is average wages before deductions. If an employee's normal working hours are the same every week and the pay is the same every week, a week's pay is that which he or she would receive if working a normal week.

If an employee's pay varies according to his or her output, but working hours are always the same each week, a week's pay is worked out by multiplying the number of hours worked each week by the average hourly pay worked over the last week's employment. Each year there is a maximum entitlement an employee can claim for a week's pay for redundancy purposes. The Department of Employment, trade union or low pay unit can advise and assist in calculating this amount.

THE RIGHT TO TIME OFF TO LOOK FOR OTHER WORK

Employees with a minimum of two years continuous service have the right to paid time off work to look for another job. Employees without this amount of service should still be allowed time off to look for other work if they have been selected for redundancy.

FURTHER READING

Attwood, M. *Personnel Management* Macmillan Professional Masters, 1989
Brewster, C. & S. Connock, *Industrial relations: cost effective strategies* Hutchinson, 1986
Edwards, M. *Dismissal law: a practical guide for managers* Kogan Page, 1991
Lewis, P. *Practical employment law: a guide for human resource managers* Blackwell, 1992
Stewart, A. & V. Stewart, *Managing the poor performer* Gower, 1982

INVESTING IN TRAINING

There can be little doubt that industry and the world of work is getting more complex. This is made clear in the amount of paperwork associated with even the most minor company details. Legal measures covering health and safety, equal opportunities and data protection have generated a huge increase in the workload and working practices in the majority of organisations. The wealth of information can often test even the most qualified member of staff. Needless to say, it is virtually impossible for even the most well-prepared employee to glean all the information he or she needs to know about a workplace in the time allocated for a job interview, or indeed, in an hour's discussion with his or her supervisor on day one.

E X E R C I S E

> Make a list of all the information a future employee may like to find out about an organisation he or she is applying to. Some aspects of business life are covered by national laws which set down minimum standards, others are unique to each company. Divide the list into national (or formal) and local (or informal) rules and regulations.

The single European market inevitably means that business processes will be more complex in future. Large organisations require a multipurpose information system able to cope with all the details associated with several business tasks. The ability of business systems to collect and disseminate information will increase as the complexity of inter-European businesses increases. Here are three of the possible reasons why:

- the continued growth of international networks will involve much cooperation and exchange of different information on, for example, standards, requirements, products, services, company laws and qualifications;
- the convergence of different businesses, cultures, working methods, in the design of products and in the provision of services will mean an increase in the amount of information needed to assist in decision making;
- safety, equality and environmental issues are regarded as far more significant today than ever before. A necessary outcome of this will be an increase in information on minimum standards to comply with the law.

THE INDUCTION PERIOD

Induction periods are often regarded as costly investments, but there are advantages for both employers and employees. It is essential therefore that both parties have important details available for easy and ready reference. No matter the size or nature of a company, the long-term benefits in both time and money cannot be over-emphasised. Some of these benefits are discussed below.

TIME SAVING

It takes time to plan and conduct an induction programme. Time especially put aside to plan a good induction programme is a good investment because it can effectively be copied or repeated each time a new recruit is employed. Although an induction programme has to be reviewed and updated in the light of any changes in the workplace, the bulk of the preparation can be a 'one-off' task. In terms of an employee's time, future working hours can be much better managed if he or she is familiar from the start with as much company policy and information as possible. Induction programmes should include as much information as possible about:

- Office layout and procedure
- Sick pay
- Welfare services
- Company perks
- Bonus schemes
- Equal opportunities legislation and the equal opportunities policy
- Personnel forms
- Health and safety in the workplace
- Data protection at work

CONSISTENCY AND STANDARDISATION

An induction programme eliminates the risk of inconsistency, misunderstandings and wrong interpretations arising out of confusion. It eliminates the subjectiveness of individual responses (however well intentioned they may be), and ensures that everyone receives the same information and the same answer to the same question.

THE SOCIAL FACTOR

An induction period, especially in large organisations when several new recruits may be starting together, is an ideal way of employees getting to know one another and their environment. The good staff relations that the induction programme fosters should not be overlooked. The induction period should in fact be regarded as an important and effective method of communication; just as important as any other method such as notice boards, bulletin boards, or letters. It is not enough to rely on the grapevine to supply newcomers with important and up-to-date information about a company. Although the grapevine does exist within all organisations, and can carry useful information, it may also carry inaccuracies and assumptions which can easily lead to confusion.

EXERCISE

Imagine your group has been appointed as the new personnel management team of a large new firm. The management has decided to set aside three days to provide all new employees with an induction programme. Draw up a timetabled programme to include all of the information you consider important.

GROUP INDUCTION PROGRAMMES

If organisations conduct their recruitment and selection campaigns effectively, it should be quite simple to arrange a formal induction programme at specific times of the year most appropriate to the company's calendar of activities. The group method is ideal for fostering future relationships, and ensures that newcomers feel less isolated. The friendships established help set up internal communication networks, and encourage newcomers to participate in company life.

Induction programmes should include information on company goals, objectives, plans and directions; as well as the timing and planning of company publications and departmental meetings. In this way, the induction programme acts as a useful summary of company policy and practice. Just as a firm has policies for personnel, for equal opportunities, for finance and for marketing, so too should it have policies for communication. Plenty of time should be allowed in an induction programme for employees to ask questions and to find out about the range of activities within the company.

COMPANY INDUCTION MANUALS

Ideally, induction programmes should be accompanied by induction manuals. Unfortunately, there is a tendency in many businesses to arm new recruits with bulky manuals, without providing the necessary time to read them or the support to fully understand them. A small company induction manual, carefully organised and thoughtfully written, should contain the answers to most of the questions employees are interested in. A manual should also be used in conjunction with a live induction programme in order to be of maximum benefit. Although a manual should eliminate incorrect answers, it will only do so if it is read, so time should be set aside for new recruits to read and understand the manual. Also, it is a useful idea in preparing a manual to use a spiral binder or loose leaf note book so that changes in policy or company rules, as well as information about future or past events can be inserted or replaced easily.

EXERCISE

Contact a local firm and if possible arrange a visit. Find out as much as you can about their induction procedures. Do they have a formal induction programme with sufficient time set aside, or do they simply rely on haphazard methods of information getting around on the grapevine? Also, find out about the content of the induction programme. Deliver a short talk to your group summarising what you have found out.

STAFF APPRAISAL

The function of staff appraisal is to give both employers and employees an opportunity to discuss current performance and agree a long-term work plan for future projects. Nowadays, there is a trend towards increased employee participation in overall company activities and decisions, and a reduction in the traditional hierarchical structures which in the past have created problems.

Face-to-face informal meetings between employees and supervisors can provide an invaluable opportunity to discuss all sorts of issues, which otherwise might become distorted through the grapevine mechanism. These meetings are exceptionally well suited to the setting up of a two-way communication process, and create a climate for open communication. Individuals should meet frequently, and although such meetings should be well prepared for, there should be no restrictive ground rules. One worthwhile practice which might be considered is to have minutes taken so that each item discussed is recorded by both people. This enables progress to be measured more easily at any subsequent meetings, and avoids the risk of confusion or forgetfulness by either party.

DISCUSSION POINT

All organisations have a grapevine whereby information is passed on in an informal fashion. More traditional methods of communication such as meetings are also important as a means of exchanging information, keeping up to date, and establishing a good working climate. Make two lists, call the first formal, and the second informal, and under each write out the kind of information one would normally expect to pass through an organisation in the two ways.

METHODS OF STAFF APPRAISAL

The methods used for staff appraisal should be as informal as possible, since informal situations often lead to better communication than formal situations. Notes taken under the following headings will serve as a useful memory aid.

JOB DETAILS

What are the main details and tasks which make up the job? It is important to remember that the employer's and employee's perceptions of what constitutes a particular job may differ. Therefore, it is essential that the appraisal begins by clarifying the post-holder's job and establishing what his or her main duties are and to whom they are responsible. This should also include a joint assessment of main priorities and future targets. Future targets should be based on the employee's strengths and preferences, as well as on company goals.

ACHIEVEMENTS
- What has been achieved since the last appraisal?
- What has been done well or badly?
- What goals can be set to improve achievements?

Where the major source of achievement is being derived from minor duties, then it may suggest that a job description analysis ought to be undertaken. The manager or interviewer ought to begin the assessment by concentrating on an employee's successes rather than failures. Targeting areas for improvement should not be regarded solely as the employee's task. Managers have an important role to play in identifying methods to improve performance, and the tasks of each party should be agreed upon during the appraisal. Also, other employees within the organisation who could possibly assist should be considered and consulted independently. For example, an employee who has been promoted from the job in question could be consulted to provide help and advice.

EXERCISE

Make arrangements to interview a local private or public sector human resource manager. Find out about his or her current tasks. Which tasks provide the greatest source of achievement and which the least?

OBSTACLES TO PERFORMANCE AND ACHIEVEMENT
This section can include numerous issues, which are not necessarily related to each other or, indeed, directly concerned with a post-holder's job. Obviously, most of the obstacles will be brought to the appraisal by the employee, since he or she is obviously more informed about them than a manager. However, it is important for the employer to consider possible ways in which they affect the post-holder's performance; too dictatorial, perhaps? too much pressure from above? or too ready with unrealistic demands?

The issues which may be obstacles and barriers to achievement should be addressed in an appraisal. They may include:

- Responsibilities
- Weaknesses
- Relationships with colleagues/external relationships
- Work pressure/pressure from outside of work
- Aspirations and ambitions, and hindrances to achieving them
- Priorities
- Time management and time effectiveness
- Extra curricular work such as committee meetings, union activities
- Customer contact and dealing with the public
- Telephone contact

DISCUSSION POINT

Obviously what one person considers a negative aspect of a job might well be regarded as a positive aspect by another employee. For example, some people enjoy meetings and team work, while others thrive on working alone and consider meetings to be a hindrance to their job.
    Working as a group write a list of all the positive aspects and negative aspects of a manager's job. Afterwards compare the two lists, how do they differ? What advice

would you give to a dissatisfied employee in order to reduce the obstacles and negative aspects of his or her job?

ACTION PLAN FOR CAREER DEVELOPMENT

This is the final stage in appraisal and may only take place when all other issues have been discussed. The purpose of this fourth stage is to agree upon action to be taken to improve an employee's performance and output. It may highlight specific needs to be addressed, such as:

• Lack of clarity and confusion over job description
• Coaching
• Training
• Counselling
• Who is to take such action and when they are to take it has to be identified very clearly.

DISCUSSION POINT

It could be argued that a meeting is not truly over until all agreed action to be taken is completed. Make a list of the obligations or duties a participant of a meeting has to fulfil after the meeting has finished.

Career development is an issue which should be addressed at each appraisal, since it is easy to be complacent and overlook long-term aims and ambitions which would remain unfulfilled.

Managers and interviewers have a key role to play in assisting staff in this area by encouraging them to think positively about their current and future performance. It is unhelpful to completely separate career development from personal development, since the individual's goals so frequently overlap. It is necessary to identify training needs and to set realistic targets for whatever recommendations are agreed.

EXERCISE

First design an appropriate questionnaire and then do a survey of local people to find out what they find the most and least rewarding aspects of their jobs. Next, ask what career development plans they have made, if any, to enhance their job satisfaction.

It is important to follow-up staff appraisals, since no meeting can be effective until any follow-up action has been completed. Writing up appraisals requires skill, not least because it could involve exposure of particularly sensitive issues. The aim is to record the essential steps which have been agreed, not to labour over unnecessary details. It is useful to include an action column to enter the name of the person required to take specific action. As well as accuracy, the most important aspect about appraisal notes is that they should be circulated as soon as possible after the staff appraisal has taken place.

C ASE-STUDY

A publishing company recently introduced joint appraisal training for appraisors and appraisees. The aims of this initiative were: to reduce the burden of responsibility on the managers; to allow the employee to realise they had joint responsibility for a sucessful interview; to remove any suspicions of hidden agendas which can exist when manager-only training is provided. The courses have been most enthusiastically received by managers and employees. Managers have reported easier appraisals, with more proactive and motivated staff. Training needs for skills training such as assertiveness have also been identified.

The courses are being repeated again this financial year, and are likely to be reproduced in a sister company.

SAMPLE FORMS

Job description: to be prepared by jobholder, signed by manager, countersigned by their manager

Job title: . . . .

Department: . . . .

Organisation chart: . . . .

Purpose of the job: . . . .

Key activities: . . . .

Occasional tasks: . . . .

Judgement and decision-taking: . . . .

Communications and contacts: . . . .

Innovation and flair: . . . .

Accountability for resources: . . . .

Effort and physical skill: . . . .

Background: . . . .

Appraisal form
Name: . . . .   Department: . . . .

Job title: . . . .   Division: . . . .

Date of interview: . . . .   Time in present job: . . . .

1 Achievements
List and comment on key activities of the job
(a) Key activity . . . .   Extent to which fulfilled . . . .

. . . .

2 Objectives

(a) Objectives jointly agreed at last   Extent to which fulfilled . . . .
interview

. . . .

(b) What specific objectives have been agreed over the next 12 months (and to
what standard, if measurable)? . . . .

. . . .

3 Changes

Are there any changes which would be made by the jobholder's manager or by
others within . . . . which could help the jobholder to be more effective? If
so, please elaborate.

. . . .

4 Career

What kind of job would the jobholder like to be doing in three years, or even
further ahead? (Appraiser may wish to comment) . . . .

5 Action plans

As a result of the appraisal discussion the following has been agreed:

(a) Action required is: . . . .

(i) Training courses . . . .

Subject (and likely duration)Internal or external?   Target date for
. . . . completion . . . .

(ii) Other training/experience recommended (e.g. on job coaching, project work,
committee work) . . . .

(b) No action to be taken because . . . .

6 Appraiser's comments

        Signed . . . .   Date . . . .

7 Appraisee's comments

I have read sections sections 1–6 above and wish to add the following comments (if
any)

        Signed . . . .   Date . . . .

8 Comments (if any) by appraiser's Manager

        Signed . . . .   Date . . . .

Note: a copy of this completed form should be given to the appraisee, the original
being retained by the appraiser. Both copies to be destroyed when superseded by
the next appraisal form

POSITIVE ACTION

WHAT IS POSITIVE ACTION?

Positive action is to do with the provision of equal opportunities in employment. It
is sometimes incorrectly referred to as positive discrimination. Both the Sex

Discrimination Act and the Race Relations Act allow certain forms of positive action. The main purpose of positive action is to undo the effects of past race and sex discrimination. Training organisations, employers, and trade unions may take positive action measures to encourage members of a particular group to take advantage of opportunities for participating in jobs within a particular department. In fact, the Employment Act of 1989 has broadened the scope of the Race Relations Act and positive action training can now be provided by anyone. Examples of positive action in recruitment might include the placing of job advertisements in ethnic minority newspapers to attract black applicants, or using employment agencies and careers offices in areas where high numbers of ethnic minorities live, for example, Toxteth in Liverpool and Handsworth in Birmingham.

Positive action is not only a UK based initiative. The USA has a long-established system of affirmative action, and several EC states have equivalent schemes designed to improve equal opportunities. In order to improve positive action in the workplace, it is essential that all companies first become equal opportunities employers. As we discussed in Chapter 4, an equal opportunities policy and statement of good intention are important starting points to achieve total commitment to equality. Positive action also helps focus on traditionally held assumptions about what are men's and women's jobs, and the type of experience which is really necessary to fill such jobs. For example, it may well be customary to fill middle management posts from the craft and technical department of the company, which are predominantly male, rather than from the administrative and secretarial sections which are predominantly female, even though their experience is probably just as relevant. Positive action schemes should develop training programmes designed to compensate women for past discrimination. Similarly, equivalent measures to promote ethnic minorities need to be more widely developed in the majority of organisations.

EXAMPLES OF POSITIVE ACTION

During its equal opportunities monitoring process, Beaverdale Ltd have found that, although half of its 5,000 employees are female, the women are concentrated in low-grade jobs, and only a handful are in management posts. A positive action programme entitled 'Women into Management' has been developed to increase the number of women in high grade jobs.

DISCUSSION POINT

Quite possibly, your college offers a range of positive action programmes for students. For example, are there any Women into Management groups, or women only groups, or access courses for ethnic minority students or students with disabilities? Try to find out what positive action programmes have been introduced and how successful they have been in promoting equal opportunities for disadvantaged groups.

POSITIVE ACTION IN ADVERTISING

XYZ Printers Ltd

This co-operative has an equal opportunities policy and proposes to run a special course for female operatives who wish to become qualified for promotion to inspector grade, and who are currently under-represented in our engineering workshop.

(Section 48 Sex Discrimination Act)

POSITIVE ACTION IN TRAINING

Fairplay PLC

This company is committed to providing all employees with full equality of opportunity. As part of our equal opportunities monitoring process, it has become clear that female staff and male and female staff from ethnic minorities are under-represented in middle and top management posts. Therefore, a two-week management training course for anyone from these groups will be held shortly. For further details, contact the personnel department.

Several companies are beginning to pay much more attention to older people as potential recruits. The decline in the number of school leavers entering the labour market has forced employers to advertise and recruit older workers. As soon as any particular group's needs begin to be overlooked or ignored, that group rapidly becomes a disadvantaged group. This disadvantage is sufficient reason for companies to introduce a range of positive action measures to combat the discrimination, since it represents an economic waste to ignore any employee. In the end, it will ultimately be those companies which break the mould and are prepared to broaden the concept of the traditional youth labour market who will survive.

POSITIVE ACTION PROGRAMMES IN THE UK
These include:

- Women into Management (WIM)
- Women into Science and Engineering (WISE)
- Women into Technology
- Women and Manual trades (WAMT)
- Women in Enterprise
- Women into Business
- Women's Studies

Positive action, like most issues associated with equal opportunities, has not always been highly regarded. From a classical equal rights position, some people argue that it is unfair to men or to whatever group constitutes the dominant group in a workforce (usually, white males). They also question its real effectiveness as a strategy, pointing out that it may well lower the credibility of those who benefit from it, because of peer group assumptions that under 'real' circumstances they would not actually be fit for a particular job. However, those who believe in positive action justify it either as compensation for past inequalities suffered by women, or as a very necessary measure to assure a future equal society. Given the increasing demands within minority groups for greater equality, positive action training measures seem set to remain.

DISCUSSION POINT

What do you consider to be the advantages and disadvantages of positive action programmes, for example, Women into Management, from the employee's and employer's points of view? Do you think there is a need for positive action programmes for men to encourage them into traditional female jobs such as nursery nursing, where they are under represented?

POSITIVE ACTION PROGRAMMES IN THE EC

As part of the EC Directive on equal opportunities for women, a number of new positive action programmes have been planned. Many other programmes have been running successfully since the early 1980s. New Opportunities for Women (NOW) is an EC led programme which has been designed to undo the effects of inequality in the labour market between men and women. It has also placed increased emphasis on national governments to comply with the principle of 'equal pay for work of equal value' laid down in the Treaty of Rome.

Other EC positive action measures aimed at abolishing the discrimination experienced by workers with disabilities, are also being adapted. HELIOS is an EC action programme designed to promote disabled workers in the labour market and raise awareness amongst employers of the abilities and capacities of disabled people, rather than on the negative prejudice about disability.

INTERNAL AND EXTERNAL TRAINING RESOURCES

A well-trained workforce is one of a company's best assets, since it has been proved that training is one of the main methods of achieving success. A well-trained workforce increases motivation which in turn increases productivity and output. In general terms, a well-trained workforce is a successful workforce.

On-going training is important both from the employer's and employee's points of view. In a modern economy like ours, the nature of work is constantly changing. The single European market will bring even greater change, which will be reflected throughout the world of work. More new technology appears annually, which means that new work skills are constantly required. To succeed in work, people will need to be more flexible about how and where they work, and be ready to learn new skills or to adapt the range of skills they already have to cope with the demands of new products and processes.

> Many UK companies have been criticised for spending too little of their income on staff development and training. What is likely to occur in UK trading if this trend is not reversed?

Fewer people in future will finish their working lives in the same industry or career in which they started. It is probably also true to argue that few people will be able to rely on a single training course at the outset of their working lives to keep them employable throughout their working lives. The variety and range of training courses currently available provides evidence to support this trend.

NVQs, SVQs AND GNVQs

NVQs, SVQs and GNVQs are qualifications about work. They are based on standards of competence set by industry. They are both beneficial and vital to employers. NVQs are available to over 80 per cent of the workforce. They provide employers with the confidence that an individual holding a specific qualification can do a specific job. It is up to individuals to decide how and where they learn: at work, at college, or in their own time. NVQs will encourage more people to seek qualifications, which will lead to a better-trained, better-qualified and more efficient workforce.

ON-THE-JOB TRAINING

This is where employees and trainees develop and improve their skills and knowledge while actually performing the job in question. Certain jobs are ideally suited to on-the-job training, for example, word processor operators, fork-lift truck drivers and hairdressers. Inevitably a gradual improvement in skills occurs with constant practice.

On-the-job training has been a major feature of most government training schemes introduced over the past decade. It is based largely on learning through building up a range of practical skills by actively participating in the job itself. Several other training methods combine a mixture of on-the-job training with other forms of training. For example, traditional apprenticeships have been characterised by periods of on-the-job training combined with periods spent studying the theory at college. This form of combined training has a proven and successful track record of providing trainees with useful skills supported by a sound understanding of theory. University and polytechnic sandwich courses, most often in engineering subjects, have tended to combine learning through a mixture of on and off-the-job training.

> What types of jobs are suitable for on-the-job training? Listed below are a range of jobs. Discuss which training methods would be most appropriate for each.
>
> • Accountant
> • Vet

- Hairdresser
- Word processor operator
- Personal Assistant
- Gardener
- Engineer
- Plumber
- Carpenter
- Personnel manager

OFF-THE-JOB TRAINING

As the name implies, this type of training generally occurs outside the normal working environment. Increasingly, employers are encouraging their employees at all levels to develop their skills through external training routes. Off-the-job training methods vary, and are very often dependent on both an organisation's willingness to release staff, as well as on the availability of suitable local job training facilities. Day-release courses at local further education colleges have been a major source of off-the-job training for many years. Several occupations have in fact had their entire workforces trained to national qualification standards through the day-release method: hairdressing, construction, electrical work, plumbing, clerical, banking etc. The courses followed are broadly equivalent to those followed by students on full-time courses, though the latter are obviously more theory based and lack the practical element. Other than the government training schemes (Youth Training and Adult Training), governments also assist organisations and individuals financially. Some of the more common schemes are listed below:

- businesses in their first year may benefit from Business Growth Programmes (BGP) held out of normal office hours;
- women returner courses to paid employment;
- workers with disabilities who require assistance with rehabilitation costs and training.

Off-the-job training, perhaps more so than training undertaken on the job, is an invaluable method of ensuring employees keep up to date within their field. It also assists organisations and individuals to plan both company goals and personal career goals. Finally, it encourages an organisation to assess its future more precisely by focusing on the current and future skill requirements of the company.

THE CASE OF FOREIGN LANGUAGES

'Why bother to learn Spanish, German or French? After all many foreigners speak English.' This has been the attitude commonly held by people in business, many of whom think it is unnecessary to speak other languages, even for international trade. Some people think that because they left school without a second language they could not acquire it later. People who do business abroad know that, if they can speak the language of the country they are dealing with, they are better able to conduct their business; even a few polite phrases are better than nothing. Although they may use a professional translator for documentation, the best results are achieved if everyone can follow the translation themselves. In the UK, ways are being actively sought of combining job-oriented university courses with language training. Ideally, firms should recruit language graduates and train them in more immediately usable skills, keeping their language skills 'on hold' until needed.

E X E R C I S E

Find out what language courses are available in your area. Contact the local chamber of commerce or TEC, or go through local newspapers to see what is on offer. Carry out your research, then write an article for your group or college magazine entitled: 'The advantages of learning foreign languages'

TRAINING NEEDS AUDIT (TNA)

In general terms, a TNA is a simple means of measuring the gap between skills available and skills required in the workforce, and making recommendations to bridge the gap. The development of new training opportunities has enabled many businesses to address training as a serious issue, not as a side issue as in the past.

TNAs can either be undertaken in-house by a team of experts or an external consultancy can be brought in. Here again, government funding may be available through the local TEC. In view of the importance of maximising human potential through training, all companies should undertake a TNA at the point of recruitment planning or new product preparation. A training analysis must not be seen as an isolated event, since most aspects of business depend on the TNA achieving an accurate overview in the first place.

A TNA should gather as much information as possible about the following:

- What are the company's major and secondary products?
- Are the products likely to change to adapt to the single European market or to expand the current customer base?
- Which skills does the workforce already have?
- What other skills may they need to acquire in the future in order to continue to trade successfully?
- Would the availability of different skills enable the company to expand into the European market?
- Which foreign languages should be acquired?

E X E R C I S E

Collect as many TNA report forms as you can from large organisations. Compare the way in which each has been designed. Draw up a checklist of the factors which ought to be taken into account when designing an efficient and easy to use report form.

INVESTORS IN PEOPLE

The Investors in People standard was introduced by the Government in 1990, to act as the foundation for an action programme aimed at encouraging employers to plan, act on and review the training needs of all their employees in order to achieve business objectives. Investors in People is not simply about persuading TEC member companies to do more training. It is about helping members to realise the value of their most important investment – their own people. Investors in People has been developed nationally by business people for business people.

An Investor in People:

- makes a public commitment to actively encourage employees' development in order to achieve business objectives;
- regularly reviews the training and development needs of all employees;
- takes action to train and develop individuals on recruitment and throughout their employment;
- evaluates the investment in training and development to assess achievement and improve future effectiveness.

SOURCES OF TRAINING

Below are some of the most common sources of training an organisation might consider.

TECs

Local business-led TECs host and deliver a range of courses specific to the needs of the local economy. Organisations which apply for membership of their local TECs may benefit from:

- assistance with planning training
- obtaining grants
- finding new European business partners
- business growth programmes
- management development programmes

As well as specialised local programmes which several of the TECs offer, there are a number of national schemes which TECs are responsible for running, including the Business Growth Programme (BGP) which is aimed at small and medium-sized businesses. The programme covers several topics such as tax, VAT, recruitment and selection, selling skills, and telephone sales techniques.

EXERCISE

Contact your local TEC. Find out if any Business Growth Programmes are currently being held in your area, or if any are planned for the near future. If so, select a couple of group members to attend a session. Afterwards, the students that attended should deliver a short talk to the group outlining the course contents, and the views of any participants they had an opportunity to talk to.

RECRUITMENT AND TRAINING GRANTS

These can be worth up to £2,000 for each new employee. The grants are designed to encourage employers to provide well-structured training programmes. They need not necessarily lead to a nationally recognised qualification.

TRAINING ACCESS POINTS (TAPs)

These are computerised data bases that provide information on the range of training schemes available in a particular area, or training opportunities which are available nationally. TAPs are just one of the local information services that are provided through the TEC network.

DEPARTMENT OF EDUCATION AND SCIENCE (DES) INITIATIVES

For example, the PICK-UP Training Directory (Professional Industrial and Commercial Updating Programme). The directory lists up-to-the-minute details of over 20,000 short employment schemes available in Britain. It was introduced in the UK in 1982, and has since expanded to include a PICK-UP Europe unit which encourages inter-European partnerships. PICK-UP is administered by the Department of Education. It encourages colleges of further and higher education to increase both the quantity and quality of their training services for employers and employees alike. In general, courses are designed to meet the real needs of industry and as such are short, flexible, cost effective and may be planned and modified to meet individual or local needs. They are consumer charged: costs are met by an organisation or by individuals.

INDUSTRIAL TRAINING ORGANISATIONS (ITOs)

Industrial training boards were first set up in 1964 following the Industrial Training Act of 1964. Their main role was to provide training for people employed in, or intending to be employed in a particular industry. Now, there are over a hundred ITOs covering business sectors in which approximately 80 per cent of the UK's workforce is employed.

COLLEGES AND UNIVERSITIES

Consultancy; initial and updating training, employee secondment and exchange programmes.

OPEN LEARNING OR DISTANCE LEARNING

As a means of training this method is becoming increasingly popular as both a time-effective and flexible method of learning. Individual needs can be slotted into flexible timetables, and enable the trainee to learn at his or her own pace. The only drawback of the open learning concept is the isolation factor. Several open colleges have tried successfully to overcome this negative factor by arranging weekend seminars, lunches, conferences and other get-togethers.

EXERCISE

Ask someone you know who has been involved in an open learning course, such as an Open University degree, or a distance learning writing course. What did he or she consider to be the best and worst aspects of this type of learning?

CHAMBERS OF COMMERCE AND INDUSTRY

Two out of every five businesses employing between 20 and 2,000 are members of a chamber of commerce, and membership is growing within the small business sector.

Chambers of commerce share a number of features in common:

- they provide a range of top-quality services to the business community;
- they are owned by the business community and respond to its needs;
- they are professionally managed and run as businesses with a collective turnover of 85 million pounds;
- chambers are businesses whose funding comes from the subscriptions of members.

Chambers of commerce are part of a private-sector network which spans the world and cooperates closely with government export services. They organise trade missions and exhibitions and run seminars on trading conditions throughout the world. Chambers of commerce are the gateway to advice on employment law. They can also help advise an employer about local sources of information and assistance. As far as training is concerned, chambers run business courses to improve the skills of both employers and employees. They also provide import and export training to assist a company in overseas trading.

ACTIVITY

Contact your local chamber of commerce, and if possible arrange a visit. What are its main activities and its local membership rate? Many chambers publish a journal or magazine. If your local chamber does, ask to see a copy and find out what training courses are on offer. Present a summary of the magazine to your group.

For organisations who wish to provide a job placement or permanent job for trainees or students, the main sources of candidates are:

- government training programmes: the two largest programmes in the UK are youth training for young people and adult training for unemployed adults. Delivery of these training programmes is overseen by the TEC network;
- colleges and universities as well as traditional apprenticeships;
- European trainees through cross channel training programmes and exchanges undertaken via the TEC network. Also, foreign language trainees through Language Export Centres (may be contacted through the local TEC), as well as through the long-established exchange programmes which are common within higher education.

FURTHER READING

Anderson, A. *Successful training practice: a managers guide to personnel development* Blackwell, 1992

Fowler, A. *A good start: effective employee induction* Institute of Personnel Management, 1983

Goodworth, C. *The secrets of successful staff appraisal and counselling* Heinemann, 1989

Kenney, J. & M. Reid *Training interventions* Institute of Personnel Management, 1986

7

PERSONNEL RECORDS AND DATA PROTECTION

All organisations keep records, whatever their size or the nature of their business. Each company is different and so too is the information which it stores. In general, business information can be grouped under one of the following headings:

- products and service information
- customer and client details
- future prospects, such as possible new customers and products
- laws and regulations such as health and safety guidelines, equal opportunities literature and EC regulations.

PERSONNEL RECORDS

Apart from these records, all organisations keep another type of information; information about staff, both the existing workforce as well as records of past employees and potential employees who have applied for jobs. This information is referred to as personnel records. A lot of it is related to the company as a whole and does not contain specific details about individual members of staff. For example, statistics on labour turnover for the past five years. These statistics may only involve individual employees names when it is used to analyse the reason why people have left the company. For instance, during monitoring of the equal opportunities policy, to check that an employee did not leave because of discrimination.

Personnel records are kept in a number of organisations under the following headings:

- Absenteeism
- Sickness
- Grade of job and position in grade
- Staff appraisals
- Probation report
- Annual leave entitlements
- References from past employers
- Pension contributions to company pension schemes
- Information relating to disciplinary matters

- Financial details relating to salaries and wages
- Personal details such as age, marital status, number of dependants and other items of a personal nature which might have been supplied on an employee's job application form.

ABSENTEEISM

This usually relates to the entire workforce and includes specific details about staff absences. Information such as the total number of days off and the reasons why are generally kept. In the event of a high number of absences an individual may be asked for an explanation during a staff appraisal interview. Extra bonuses are sometimes provided for staff who have very few absences, and in contrast, they may be removed in the event of high absenteeism.

SICKNESS

Details about staff sickness and special arrangements for employees with disabilities are kept.

JOB GRADE

An employee's job grade, and the length of time in the grade.

STAFF APPRAISALS

Information about the appraisal is usually kept by the personnel department and referred to at future appraisal interviews. This information relates to the discussions which have taken place and the action which has been agreed upon.

PROBATION REPORT

Since new staff in almost all businesses are subject to a probation period of 26 weeks from the date of appointment, confirmation of appointments are usually subject to a satisfactory report on service and performance. These reports are kept for future references, appraisals etc.

ANNUAL LEAVE

This varies between employees, often on the basis of the scale or grade of job, or length of service. It is common for higher grade posts to have increased holiday entitlements than staff on lower grades. Also, in certain circumstances the entitlement is increased in recognition of long service.

REFERENCES

Usually from past employers or educational institutions.

PENSIONS

Contributions which have been made in the current employment, as well as past contributions from previous employment.

FINANCIAL DETAILS

About wages, salaries, and any bonus or incentive scheme.

DISCIPLINARY AND GRIEVANCES

Notes should always be kept of any dispute which has arisen in the past.

PERSONAL DETAILS

Although a growing number of organisations are reducing the amount of personal details they request on an application form, many still ask questions about an individual's private life and personal circumstances. Many equal opportunities employers, however, avoid asking questions which can prejudice the decision of the selection committee. Although such information might be needed for monitoring the effectiveness of the equal opportunities policy, it can be asked on a separate sheet which is not used in the selection of candidates. Remember, each candidate selected for a job should be chosen on his or her ability to do the job, not on any personal details such as marital status or childcare arrangements.

EXERCISE

If possible, arrange to visit a local employer or invite a personnel officer from a local business to your group to discuss what kinds of personnel records they keep. Ask the reasons for keeping such records. Is the information which is stored available for employees to see if they wish?

COMPUTERISED RECORDS

Today most companies use computers and computerised records. This saves a lot of space previously occupied by filing cabinets. In the same way that a filing cabinet can be locked to preserve confidentiality, a computer user has a password and non-users are not allowed to know what the password is. So, in theory at least, the information stored is treated confidentially.

EXERCISE

Carry out your research, and then write an illustrated article for your college magazine or for general readership for your group. The title is 'A short history of data processing: from paper to machines'. Your article should begin with the developments in data processing in the late 1950s.

The benefits of a computerised system include:

- huge storing capacity: computers can hold much more information than a manual system;
- they can be used for several different purposes, and at any one time by several users;
- computers are sex neutral: in the past many employers have tended to group records on the basis of blue records for male and pink for female. In an organisation such as the careers service this can lead to bad practice. For example, if a vacancy for a motor mechanic is sent in, human error and subjective opinion can lead to stereotyping and it is likely that a boy's record will be chosen above a girl's record. In a computerised system this is much less likely to happen;
- computers make it easy to sort out and extract information according to sex, age, disability which can be used in monitoring an equal opportunities programme;
- a security copy or 'back-up' of the computer disc can be kept. In the unfortunate

event of an office fire, a security copy which is kept off-site means that nothing is lost.

Assume you are the junior personnel manager of a large firm. You have been asked to make a report to your departmental manager outlining the advantages and disadvantages of a software package or a word processing package with which you are familiar. The report should be organised using appropriate headings and subheadings. You may invent any information or details necessary to enable you to write the report.

MANUAL RECORDS

- Might be an ideal system in a small or medium-sized business where only a few records are kept;
- less expensive than a computer system;
- if used properly, can be very flexible, and new information on a whole range of subjects can be inserted at any time. On a computer system, a new programme might possibly have to be developed to introduce a different set of information;
- difficult to keep a copy or back-up;
- involves little training in order for staff to use it, whereas a computer system requires a whole range of keyboard skills and word processing skills in order for it to be used effectively.

Arrange to visit a local employer. Find out if their personnel records are kept on computer or in a manual filing system. What do you think are the advantages and disadvantages of each system:
a for a large employer
b for a small employer

DATA PROTECTION

The Data Protection Act was introduced in 1984. The Act grew out of public concern about personal privacy in the face of sophisticated computer technology. It did not come into operation until 1987. The new law provided new rights for individuals and demands good computer practice in handling information about people.

The Act also enabled the UK to comply with EC laws. In fact, the Act owed more to pressure from the EC than anything else. The Council of Europe Data Protection Convention required that all member countries which signed the convention had to withhold the transmission of information to countries which had no laws to protect it.

British firms had started to lose overseas contracts which involved the swapping of information, because European businesses were not allowed to deal with firms in countries which could not guarantee confidentiality of computerised information. The Act requires all companies which process or use computerised personal data to register with the Data Protection Registrar.

THE PRINCIPLES OF DATA PROTECTION

Once a user is registered, the company must abide by the eight Data Protection Principles of good practice which are contained within the Act. Briefly, these state that personal data must be:

1 Obtained and processed fairly and lawfully.
2 Held only for the lawful purposes which have been described in the data user's register entry.
3 Used only for those purposes, and disclosed only to those people described in the register entry.
4 Adequate and relevant in relation to the purposes for which the information is held. In other words, the details which are held should be concise and not excessive.
5 Accurate, and where necessary always kept up to date.
6 Held no longer than is necessary for the registered purpose.
7 Accessible to the person concerned who has the right to have information about themselves corrected or taken out if they wish.
8 Surrounded by proper security, to ensure that the information does not become available to non-users.

WHAT THE ACT COVERS

The Act is concerned with 'personal data' which is 'automatically processed'. Its major defect is that it applies only to computerised information: data users who wish to breach every clause in the Act can do so with a manual system. In general, the Act works in two ways:

- by giving individuals certain rights;
- by making sure that those who use and record personal information on computers are open and honest about the use, and follow the practices laid down in the Data Protection Act.

WHAT IS PERSONAL DATA?
Personal data includes any information about named individuals. This need not be especially personal information, it can be as little as a name and address.

WHAT DOES AUTOMATICALLY PROCESSED MEAN?
This means information which is processed by a computer. It does not cover information which is held and processed manually, for example, in ordinary filing cabinets.

To completely understand the Data Protection Act it is important to know two other data protection definitions:

data users: those who control the contents and use of a collection of personal data. This can be any company, large or small, within the private or public sector;
data subject: the individuals to whom the personal data relates.

Clearly, many people are both data users and data subjects. In the course of your job you may well keep records about people such as application forms, sick notes and references. Similarly, when you join the local library or squash club, you too supply personal information such as name and address, and in so doing become a data subject.

EXERCISE

> Draw up a checklist of the situations in which you are or have been a data user and a data subject. As a data subject, what kind of information have you been asked to supply?

REGISTRATION

With very few exceptions any company which holds or controls personal data on computer must register with the Data Protection Registrar. The registrar is an independent officer appointed by Her Majesty the Queen, and reports directly to parliament. The registrar's duties include:

- setting up and maintaining a register of data users and computer bureaux and making it publicly available;
- encouraging, where appropriate, the development of codes of practice to help data users comply with the principles of data protection;
- considering breaches of the Act, and, where appropriate, prosecuting offenders.

Registration is normally for three years and one standard fee is payable to cover this period. Data users and computer bureaux who do not register are committing a criminal offence. The penalty for non-registration can be a fine of up to £2,000 in the magistrates court, or an even bigger fine in the High Court.

A DATA USER'S REGISTER ENTRY
A register entry is compiled from the information given in the registration application form. The entry gives the data user's name, address and broad descriptions of:

- the personal data held;
- the purpose for which it is stored and used;
- the source from which the information may be obtained;
- the people to whom the information may be disclosed;
- any overseas countries to which the data might be sent.

WHAT THE DATA PROTECTION ACT MEANS TO INDIVIDUALS

The Data Protection Act allows each person to have access to information held about him or herself on computer, and where appropriate to be corrected or deleted. This is known as the 'subject access right' and it means that you are entitled, on making a written request to a data user, to be supplied with a copy of any personal data held about you.

ACCESS TO THE REGISTER

The Data Protection Register is open to public inspection at the Registrar's office in Wilmslow, Cheshire. A register entry only shows what a data user is registered to do, it does not show whether or not that data user holds personal information about you

COMPLAINTS AND COMPENSATION

If a person considers that there has been a breach of one of the data protection principles, he or she is entitled to complain to the Data Protection Registrar. Also, an individual is entitled to seek compensation through the courts if damage has been caused by the loss, or unauthorised disclosure of personal data.

HOW MUCH IMPACT HAS THE DATA PROTECTION ACT HAD?

Research has shown that many organisations, small businesses especially, are still not aware of the Data Protection Act and how it applies to them. The ever-increasing range of computer technology means that the majority of businesses fall within the scope of the Data Protection Act. To encourage more people to register and find out about their obligations under the Act, the Data Protection Registrar has produced an information pack on the Act. The pack and campaign theme is called 'Ignorance is no defence'.

The EC has proposed a new Directive on Data Protection. If it becomes law it will place more restrictions on the transfer of data. The use of personal information would be outlawed unless individuals gave express permission. The transfer of data from one source to another would similarly be restricted. From the point of view of individual privacy, the new directive will certainly increase the emphasis placed on confidentiality. However, for businesses which rely on the transfer of data the new directive could create restrictions and possible problems. Companies which do a lot of direct marketing, market research, distance selling or buying will be affected most if the directive becomes law. Some of the things they will not be able to do include:

- use computer profiling to analyse personal data held by a company;
- target to any degree of accuracy a market for goods and services;
- mail people on the company's database without the express consent of the individuals concerned;
- transmit data held in computer systems within Europe to any other continent.

DISCUSSION POINT

What are the advantages and disadvantages of increased data protection and privacy from the point of view of the employer and from the employee's point of view? What are the advantages and disadvantages of a Data Protection Act?

8

GRIEVANCE AND
DISCIPLINARY PROCEDURES

In the day-to-day context of employee relations things may occasionally go wrong. Employee relations has a continuous bearing on almost all relations. After all, it is the central human element without which a company would cease to exist. There are times in most organisations when employee relations come to the forefront:

- around the annual pay talks;
- in the event of a large number of redundancies;
- during a serious industrial dispute (serious disputes are, in fact, rare and fairly minor in the context of the overall economy within the UK);
- a major alteration in working practices.

For most people employee relations are a vital part of the background to their job; but only rarely do they become a major issue. However, for some individuals employee relations are much more than background material, since their prime task is to do with the smooth running of the most important components of an organisation: its people. For these specialists it is a full-time job. Large organisations generally have specialists who deal exclusively with employee relations. The title might vary (personnel manager, staff manager, human resource specialist, office administration manager, industrial relations specialist), and the job may differ depending on the size and sector of the organisation for which they work. In general the specialist handles all people-related tasks, especially:

- Meetings and negotiations with trade unions
- Interviewing and selection
- Dismissals and grievances

EXERCISE

Think about a company with which you are familiar. Try and arrange to carry out a job study on the personnel manager or industrial relations specialist. How much time is spent on employee relations? What sort of issues does he or she deal with?

When problems arise in the workplace between managers and employees they are referred to as grievances. Depending on the size and nature of an organisation, various procedures exist to handle grievances. Individuals may go through formal channels to sort out their problems, and in most companies there are elected representatives to support and help an employee. In some workplaces these arrangements are informal. Ideally, employee representatives should be free to talk to managers about any issue arising at almost any time.

Some of the major problems associated with informal approaches tend to be:

- differences (created by misunderstandings or subjective interpretations) in the way staff are treated in different departments and by different managers;
- uncertainty and inconsistency about what the rules actually are, who makes them and how enforceable they are;
- lack of clarity over who is responsible for implementing rules and standards;
- concern on the part of those who have been elected as representatives, when they see problems solved out of their control and without their consent and involvement.

D ISCUSSION POINT

What other problems can you think of that might arise where no formal procedures for handling grievances exist?

In order to comply with the law and to avoid confusion over related issues, most organisations employing any substantial number of employees have developed formal systems for handling grievances in the workplace. According to the British Workplace Industrial Survey 1980–1984, an estimated 90 per cent of British workplaces now have formal disciplinary procedures. If an organisation employs 20 or more workers it must give, in a written statement, details of any disciplinary rules, or a reference to where these can be found, and the person whom the employee can contact if they are not satisfied with the disciplinary decision. Regardless of the number of people employed, it is highly desirable that disciplinary rules are made clear to everyone. This enables employees to understand what is expected of them in matters such as:

- Health and safety
- Timekeeping
- Race and sex discrimination
- Conduct and behaviour
- Work performance
- Use of company property
- Equal opportunities policy

It is also important to give examples of behaviour which will be regarded as gross misconduct. Put simply, this is a serious offence which normally leads to an employee's dismissal without notice. Many employers regard offences such as theft, fraud or assault as gross misconduct, but depending on the circumstances, a minor offence may constitute gross misconduct. To help employers, ACAS have produced a code of practice on disciplinary procedures in employment which outlines important issues step by step. Employers are strongly advised to follow the ACAS recommendations, which although not legally binding, may be taken into account by an industrial tribunal.

FORMAL AGREEMENT PROCEDURES

There are two main types of agreement which occur in most large organisations. These are:

SUBSTANTIVE AGREEMENTS

These concern the actual terms and conditions of employment, for example, pay, holidays, hours of work, overtime rates, fringe benefits, bonus schemes, pension arrangements, sick leave and sick pay.

PROCEDURAL AGREEMENTS

These are about the rules of negotiation and grievance. You could compare them, for instance, with the Football Association's rules for football, the Lawn Tennis Association for tennis, or the British Amateur Gymnastics Association for gymnastics. Amongst the procedural agreements there are a variety of different types and some are explained below.

DISCIPLINARY
(Includes both fair and unfair dismissal.) These procedures are almost always started by management. Disciplinary procedures are about the behaviour of individuals in the workplace. (For more information about unfair dismissal see Chapter five.)

GRIEVANCE
In general, a grievance procedure is started by a single employee. Grievance procedures are to do with any problems that an individual may have concerning the way he or she is treated at work. It might be an isolated problem which has only occurred once, or a series of problems which culminate in a grievance.

DISPUTES
In general, disputes are commenced by a union representative such as a shop steward. Dispute procedures are the collective version of grievance procedures, when, for example, several employees share a concern over the same issue.

NEGOTIATING
Negotiating procedures are initiated by a trade union (or unions if the workforce is represented by more than one). Formal negotiations rely on a variety of opinions and viewpoints before a decision is reached. By definition, negotiating involves at least two sides, usually managers and unions with several other interested parties in the background. Negotiation in the wider sense means any activity which involves two way communication: purchasing, trading, business meetings and interviewing. In employee relations it is usually to do with discussions over the terms and conditions of employment such as pay, holidays, and annual leave entitlements.

CONSULTATION

This process is generally initiated by management. Consultation procedures are the means by which the management informs employees about an issue and considers their views before reaching a decision. Consultation procedures are fair since they involve everyone's feelings rather than merely the opinion of a few. Participation in decision making helps:

- to encourage employees to accept responsibility;
- everyone to identify with company aims and objectives;
- to encourage participation in company life;
- foster cooperation, which in turn, improves the working climate.

REDUNDANCY

Almost always initiated by management. Redundancy procedures occur when management decides that it has to reduce the number of employees in the workforce. In the event of such a decision, other procedures (such as negotiation or consultation) also have an important part to play, since the management is obliged to inform unions and staff before any final decisions are reached.

EXERCISE

Working in twos, research one of the procedures described above. Write a summary of its major features for distribution among your group.

Whichever procedure is in operation in an organisation it needs to be worthy of belief. This means that employees need to regard it as being reasonably fair and reflect the needs of the majority of the workforce. If procedures are clearly defined and precisely written, life can be much easier for everyone involved. Appropriate procedures, skillfully used, can do a lot to avoid heated disputes arising out of unnecessary misunderstandings.

EXERCISE

Find out what the arrangements are for handling each of the six main procedures outlined above in an organisation you are familiar with, or arrange to visit a local firm. Make a note of:

- which procedures are written down and where they are written;
- the range of issues that are dealt with and how often they occur;
- who is involved;
- how they were elected;
- what their main responsibilities are;
- whether there is an external agent in the process (such as the local branch of the trade union, consultants or wage councils).

In order to get a clear picture it might be useful to discuss these issues with a senior manager, personnel manager or shop steward.

The range and form of procedures is endless. What might be an excellent procedure for a small organisation to adopt might be of little use in a large organisation.

Workplaces vary, not only in the types of procedure they follow but also between who is involved in any negotiations. On the management side it might be:

- The managing director
- A departmental manager
- Personnel manager
- Equal opportunities specialist
- Industrial relations specialist

On the union side it might be:

- An individual employee
- Shop steward
- Full-time union official
- A local union branch officer

Collective procedures are those in which management and unions meet to discuss and try to resolve disputes which concern all of the workforce. The success of these procedures largely depends on an organisation's employee relations policy, so it is crucial that a policy is well thought out and well managed.

GRIEVANCE PROCEDURES

WHAT IS A GRIEVANCE?

When the relationship between an employee and his or her employer is unsatisfactory to the employee, then he or she is said to have a grievance. A grievance can arise over just about any issue, for example:

- Pay
- Working conditions
- Colleagues
- Unrealistic pressure from management

When an employee has a grievance, there are several ways in which he or she can express it. How they do so is probably more to do with an individual's character than the organisation they work for. If the grievance is serious enough or occurring repeatedly, they may decide to leave the organisation. However, when the economy is in recession this may be an unrealistic thing to do, since the chances of finding another job are severely reduced. Also, leaving a job can be a difficult choice in itself, especially if the employee concerned is well paid and generally well respected and otherwise very happy in his or her work.

It goes without saying that unhappy employees are ultimately doing both themselves and the organisation they work for a disservice. Discontented employees are more likely to be uncooperative, disruptive, rude to customers, abrupt with colleagues, less productive and unrepresentative of the company.

EXERCISE

Think about a situation you have been unhappy in (for instance a particular lesson at school, a job, a journey). List 10 adjectives to describe your behaviour, together with 10 effects your behaviour is likely to have had on the people around you.

HANDLING A GRIEVANCE

In contrast to collective procedures between managers and unions about issues which affect everyone, grievance and disciplinary measures are about an individual employee's problems. They apply to every organisation which employs people. Employees are occasionally dissatisfied with events in the workplace. Problems and disagreements may result from the action, or lack of action, over an issue by an employer, manager, supervisor, or individual employee. Most employers develop a grievance procedure to cope with these problems when they arise. The procedure is written down and made clear to employees so that they know how to make a complaint, know that it will be taken seriously and properly investigated. A grievance procedure enables employees to present their case to the employer through an open and structured route.

A grievance procedure can be used to deal with complaints about a wide range of things. ACAS have recommended that the following points should be followed when drawing up a procedure:

- it should contain no more than two stages. First, the issue should be raised with the immediate supervisor and then, if there is no agreement, it should be raised directly with the employer;
- in the second stage the employee should be allowed to be represented by a colleague or by a trade union representative.
- the procedure should ensure a speedy solution to the problem. Clearly, each organisation's circumstances will affect the length of time taken, but in general most firms ought to be able to complete both stages within seven working days.

Grievances and problems in the workplace are ideal breeding grounds for disruption, which can have unfortunate results if not resolved So, it is to both the employee's and management's advantage to have a formal grievance procedure in place through which people should be encouraged to raise their grievances. A proper mechanism enables problems to be sorted out in a fairly straightforward and clear manner. Sometimes, merely allowing individuals the opportunity to air their grievances is all that is needed to improve the situation. Even if a problem can never be solved, it almost always helps matters if an employee can see that it has been taken seriously.

The law in the UK requires employers to give employees a written statement which informs them how they may take up a grievance. Although grievance procedures differ between organisations, what is important is that a system exists in all business sectors whatever their size or nature. The range of procedures varies enormously. The Department of Employment is a good role model since it has a very detailed agreement and a long tradition of dealing with grievance cases in a very structured and formally organised way. The advantage of a well-structured method is that it ensures that everyone in the workplace is aware of the process they may go through in the event of a grievance. It also reduces the chance of misunderstandings arising out of confusion.

The main points to note about grievance procedures are:

- the first crucial step in almost all grievance procedures is for the employee concerned to raise the issue with their immediate boss. ACAS recommends that the meeting between an employee and manager be recorded in writing, to guard against future memory lapses or differences in interpretation;
- the level of management and union involvement is clearly stated at each stage in the process. An employee with a grievance should be notified immediately if any changes in personnel involved in the case take place;
- there should be an in-built system or safety net to call upon in the event of management and unions failing to reach an agreement. This stage is usually referred to as an external or third-party stage. The role of the third party is to intervene in order that negotiations may continue when the other two parties have reached deadlock in talks;
- ideally, each organisation should have an open-door policy which ensures that any individual can approach senior managers about problems at any time. This enables employees to make known their feelings about the workplace. In a nutshell: if employees feel that they are able to talk openly to managers, their perception about their own status is strengthened.

EXERCISE

Try to obtain a copy or outline of a grievance procedure, if possible from an organisation you already know quite well. If you are planning to go on work experience, find out which documents contain the grievance procedure. Compare and contrast each company's procedure.

DISCIPLINARY PROCEDURES

As we have seen, grievances occur when the relationship between an employee and management is proving to be unsatisfactory to the employee. In contrast, when the relationship is proving to be unsatisfactory to the management, there may be a case for disciplinary action.

Like grievance issues, there are several ways of handling disciplinary matters. The important element again is that matters are solved as quickly and effectively as possible. A dissatisfied manager may be all too ready to dismiss a poor employee, but this in itself is a costly and time-consuming exercise since a replacement will have to be recruited and there is no guarantee that the new recruit will be an improvement. It is far better to get to the root of the problem, and if necessary, transfer an employee to another department or a different job.

To avoid disciplinary problems arising in the first place, three strategies are worth considering:

1 Well-designed training and induction programmes.
2 New challenges, for example, an employee may be under or overstretched in a particular job so a transfer may be suitable.
3 Suitable disciplinary procedures clearly written down for all parties to see, so that everyone knows from day one what is expected of them and what the result of any bad behaviour might lead to.

Disciplinary measures do not necessarily have to be seen as a form of punishment for wrongdoing. Instead, they should be regarded as an opportunity for both the manager and employee to take some form of mutually agreed corrective action. Instant dismissal is a highly unpleasant and costly activity for all parties.

In general, all disciplinary procedures should include the following 10 points:

1 There should be written procedures on disciplinary matters. This help everyone focus on the same information, based on fact rather than fiction.
2 Written details should specify exactly to whom they apply.
3 The procedure should be structured in a way that will ensure that matters are dealt with quickly. If necessary, time limits could be placed on each stage in the process to avoid undue delay.
4 The disciplinary actions which may be taken should be written clearly and precisely so that there is absolutely no chance of individuals getting a wrong impression.
5 Specify the management level which has the authority to take the various forms of disciplinary action.
6 Individuals should be allowed and encouraged to state their case, in writing as well as verbally if necessary. Also, the procedure should be constructed in such a way that an employee has plenty of opportunity to find out all the details about their alleged misbehaviour.
7 Individuals undergoing disciplinary procedures should always have the right to be accompanied to any disciplinary hearing by a trade union representative or another person of their choice.
8 All disciplinary procedures should ensure that no individuals are dismissed for a first breach of discipline. Simply from a humanitarian stance, everyone should be allowed to make one mistake without the threat of instant dismissal. However, in cases of gross misconduct, this course of action may be unavoidable.
9 Any disciplinary action taken as a result of a disciplinary procedure should not occur until such time as the case has been thoroughly investigated, with a third party brought in if necessary.
10 All disciplinary procedures should contain the right of appeal against unfavourable decisions. If a company has no appeals procedure, or if it is inadequate, this may go against them if one of their employees takes the claim to court for unfair dismissal.

EXERCISE

Consider an organisation which you know well, or arrange to visit a local company.
What sort of disciplinary procedures does it have and how effective are they?
Present a report of your findings to your group.

TRADE UNIONS

THE BACKGROUND TO TRADE UNIONS

The UK was the first country to industrialise and the first to witness conflicts between employers and employees. With little formal protection available to employees, it became increasingly obvious that they had to work together as a unified group in order to improve their working conditions and gain the attention of policy makers. It was from this stance that trade unions were formed.

During the nineteenth century the unions fought many battles to establish the right to deal collectively with employers. It is worth remembering that in the early days of industrialisation, collective action was actually against the law. It was eventually given legal recognition in the Trade Union Act 1871 and later in the Conspiracy and Protection of Property Act 1875. These Acts officially recognised trade unions for the first time, and also allowed the unions to picket peacefully. The new laws also enabled other trade unions to develop. The main interest of a trade union both then and now is in the terms and conditions of employment of its members. It negotiates these terms with employers and management.

Since British trade unions expanded and changed in response to industrial growth, it is not surprising that nowadays they are characterised by a diverse range of activities. Originally, many unions were formed out of the basis of a common skill: engineering, shipbuilding, toolmaking, mining etc. As different types of work gradually started to become unionised – teachers, journalists, etc. – more unions were created.

EXERCISE

Invite a local trade union official in the industrial sector to give a talk to your group about his or her union's perspective of current trends in the world of work.

EMPLOYERS' ASSOCIATIONS

In response to the development of trade unions by the workers, employers felt the need to organise themselves into employers' associations in order to ensure that they would be represented equally in future negotiations. In view of the many stormy events which had occurred in the first stages of collective bargaining, it was necessary for both sides to be represented equally. One of the main jobs of employers' associations is to regulate and control relations between employers and workers. In general, employers from the same or similar industries (engineering or ship building for instance) get together to negotiate the terms and conditions they will collectively offer to workers in that particular industry. Employers' associations present a united front to meet the unions. Again, like the unions, there is a wide range of employers' associations (some are known as employers' federations) and they deal with a wide range of issues. A further explanation of these organisations can be found on p. 124.

THE STRUCTURE OF A TRADE UNION

Although all trade unions have head offices and general secretaries, in practice most union members are integrated only very loosely and informally into the overall structure of their union. However, individual members within an organisation may become actively involved in the formal structures of their union in a number of key ways:

- getting elected as shop steward or employee representative, and attending local branch meetings;
- attending meetings or national conferences;
- liaising with other unions about joint incentives and services, for example, childcare services and holiday schemes.

EXERCISE

Select a member of your group to interview a NALGO union official. He or she should try to find out as much as possible about the kind of issues and problems involved in the job. Collect the information together, and prepare a short talk summarising your discussions to present to the rest of the group.

THE ROLE OF A TRADE UNION

Unions have several functions, the key tasks of one union representative in one industry might vary significantly from another union. Similarly, the role of the paid union official is very different from the unpaid official or shop steward. Whatever an individual's role is, he or she is primarily responsible for carrying out the union's policy. It should be remembered that these officials do not actually make the policy. In all unions the top policy making group consists of a body of ordinary members who meet to discuss and agree upon policy. Sometimes they consist of national groups who meet at a national conference. Others are smaller committees, but again made up of ordinary members.

The key tasks of large unions are:

- to negotiate on behalf of union members with management. Negotiations can really be about anything, and again topics for negotiation are bound to vary between organisations and sectors within an industry. The main terms and conditions which cross industrial boundaries are pay, pension rights, hours of work and employment contracts;

- the union representative has a duty to assist individual members with problems. He or she may also be asked to accompany a union member to a disciplinary hearing, or offer them advice and practical help over a grievance they may have;
- to advise on a broad range of issues such as health and safety at work, equal opportunities in the workplace, training courses and seminars etc. Several unions have developed highly successful training programmes for their industries on a wide range of topics. In addition, the majority of unions publish their own magazines and newspapers to inform members of developments and services offered to them through their membership subscriptions.

EXERCISE

Why do many people wish to join a trade union? Write down five reasons why you might consider joining a union, and five reasons why you would not. If a union negotiates for a good pay increase, do you think it is fair that non-members receive the increase when they have not supported the union?

CLOSED SHOP

A closed shop exists when all employees are required to belong to a union. Closed shops have been the subject of much controversy and debate and there has never been a complete acceptance by all workers of the notion of the closed shop. In the 1980s, the law was changed, and it is now unlawful to enforce a closed shop.

The arguments for a closed shop include:

- trade unions fight to obtain benefits and rights for members. A closed shop ensures that all who get the benefit of union work (pay increases, extra holidays, better bonuses, etc) contribute to the union. In short, there are no freeloaders. Why, it is sometimes argued, should non-members benefit when they do not subscribe to the union?
- the closed shop ensures that the union is fully representative and makes it easier for unions to exercise power with management and control over members;
- it prevents poaching by other unions simply because there are no new members for them to recruit. Loyalty is also likely to be greater, a crucial element in union strength;
- it ensures that disciplinary and grievance procedures are the same for all staff.

On the other hand, in the case against the closed shop, it is argued that:

- compulsory trade union membership is basically unfair and undemocratic since it ignores an individual's free choice. After all, it is argued, individuals ought to have the right to join or not to join an organisation as they wish;
- it can lead to bad equal opportunities practice for some individuals, who, because of their beliefs, cannot get a job in a given organisation which insists upon operating a closed shop;
- pre-entry closed shops restrict an employer's right to decide who he or she will employ in the best interests of the organisation. A post-entry closed shop, that is,

one which does not require a job applicant to be already a member of a particular union, but only to join on being recruited to the company, is less restrictive. In short, closed shops are criticised for restricting the mobility of labour.

EXERCISE

Apart from the arguments for and against the closed shop discussed above, write down three other arguments against the closed shop and three in its favour. Since the 1980s, as we have seen, enforcing a closed shop is unlawful. What do you think? Should they be allowed or not? Can you think of a better system?

THE TRADES UNION CONGRESS (TUC)

There are around 400 trade unions in the UK with around 10 million members. Clearly, the total membership figure changes continuously as new members join and existing members leave. 'Trade union density' is an expression used to describe the percentage of the working population which belongs to a trade union. Although membership varies substantially between different industries, Britain is still a country in which many working people are trade union members.

Throughout Europe, the UK is an exception to the general rule in so far as it has a single umbrella organisation like the TUC responsible for many union members. In other countries, much smaller numbers are represented by national federations or associations, and these are often split further along occupational, political, cultural or religious lines. In contrast, the British TUC includes all the major unions as well as many of the medium-sized ones. The primary aim of the TUC is to act as a mouthpiece for the unions and it is a powerful organisation which influences the government. It meets once a year, usually in September at a seaside resort, to set policy and priorities for the following year.

INDUSTRIAL TRIBUNALS

An industrial tribunal is a relatively informal 'court'. An industrial tribunal hearing usually takes place near to where an individual lives or works. Disputes arising out of statutory provisions which provide rights for workers are usually settled by industrial tribunals. Industrial tribunals were established by Parliament in 1965. They consist of a leading chairperson and two members of the public called 'side people', who have experience in industry and commerce. In practice, one of the side people represents the employee and the second represents management. Individuals can either present their own case, or for example, in the case of sex discrimination, seek help from the Equal Opportunities Commission. Industrial tribunals try to ensure that all cases are processed as quickly and cheaply as possible and provides a more informal approach to problem solving than many systems under the law.

The range of subjects covered by industrial tribunals (known as their jurisdiction) is increasing and covers a wide range of subjects including:

• Unfair dismissal

- Redundancy and redundancy payments
- Suspension on medical grounds
- Trade union membership and activities
- Maternity rights
- Equal pay
- Sex discrimination
- Race discrimination
- Pay and itemised pay statements
- Time off: for union duties, public duties such as jury service or to find new employment after being issued with a redundancy notice
- Antenatal appointments

If an industrial tribunal reaches a settlement in favour of an employee it can take one or all of the following courses of action:

- make an order declaring his or her rights;
- order that he or she be paid compensation: this could include lost earnings, travel expenses and compensation for injury to feelings;
- make a recommendation to the organisation or employer complained against to take a specific course of action within a given time to remedy the situation. For example, to consider the employee for promotion within the next six months, or to be placed on a higher pay scale.

An individual who is not satisfied with the decision taken at an industrial tribunal can appeal to the Employment Appeal Tribunal (EAT), but only on a point of law. These are conducted along similar lines to the industrial tribunal. The EAT must be given written notice of the appeal within 42 days of the date on which the tribunal decision is sent to the aggrieved employee.

EXERCISE

For this exercise, three members of your group will represent officials on an industrial tribunal panel. Other group members will represent either employers or employees and act as the jury in the following case:

GRAHAM BLANCHE vs. SKIMP DALE CORPORATION

Graham has been working in the marketing department of Skimp Dale Corporation for eight years, and has passed all relevant examinations for the job. The company have recently advertised for an international marketing officer to be in charge of departments in Madrid, Venice and Budapest. The post involves a lot of travel and periods of time spent away from home. Graham applied for the job but was not even selected for the first interview, although a number of colleagues with far fewer qualifications and less experience were. Graham noticed that all those selected for interview were single people with no children. Graham is married with three children. The tribunal you have set up must decide, after questioning the two parties, on the rights and wrongs of the case and the course of action which you think should follow.

9

EFFECTIVE PEOPLE MANAGEMENT

Work is more than the sum of money brought home at the end of the week or month. If money was the only goal, most millionaires would finish working, but in reality most continue to work. In fact, when people are asked if they would carry on working if they were to win a million pounds, most say they would. They may not necessarily carry on with their current job, but seek one which gives them greater job satisfaction.

Carry out research on a range of people in different jobs. Write an article for your college magazine entitled 'What makes people want to work?'.

It is a combination of factors such as pay, holiday entitlement, availability of training and relationships with colleagues and management, not to mention relationships outside work which can increase or reduce our job satisfaction. It is often difficult to separate the factors which influence job satisfaction into neat little compartments, since in practice most overlap.

Think of a job which you have done and write two lists: one detailing all the things you enjoyed about the job, and the other, all the things you disliked. On the whole, did you get more satisfaction or dissatisfaction out of your work?

Some factors which influence our overall satisfaction are of a temporary nature, such as attending a compulsory training course for a week about a subject in which you have no interest at all, while others are a permanent feature of a job. For instance, perhaps being expected to attend long and dull meetings at least three times a week might be regarded as a nuisance. A workplace, of course, is no more or less than the sum of the individuals which it comprises. So it is up to individual employees to improve their working environment by making suggestions to colleagues and management.

Management are only human and cannot be expected to notice all problems unless they are specifically brought to their attention. Temporary factors which might influence job satisfaction might include some on-site building or maintenance work, when for a short time only, the noise and disruption level is increased. In contrast, job satisfaction might remain a permanent 'high' or permanent 'low' in the lives of some people, but for many more it is a factor which alters regularly and is characterised by peaks and troughs.

CASE - STUDY

Work through this case-study and comment on the situation, with regard to:

1 The cause of the problems.
2 The effects on staff.
3 What else might the board of directors do to avoid similar problems arising in the future?

3R SYSTEMS LTD, SKELMERSDALE, LANCASHIRE
3R Systems is a medium-sized company based in Lancashire. There are two sides to the business:

- business computer consultancy and software development;
- human resource management and equal opportunities training.

Both sides are equally busy and there are times when the key staff are out for days on end. This has led to problems with some of the administrative staff who feel dissatisfied at being left on their own for long periods of time. Not surprisingly this is having a major impact on their job satisfaction. The board of directors have decided to have a meeting about this for all staff to attend. Everyone is encouraged to participate in the meeting and to share their real feelings. The main complaints are to do with staff feeling isolated for much of the time and therefore generally dissatisfied with their jobs. Various ideas are discussed at the meeting. The most popular suggestions to remedy the situation are to:

- hold regular staff socials out of normal office hours;
- introduce a system of job rotation so that everyone gets a chance to learn other skills;
- re-arrange the office so as to bring everyone closer together;
- close for an hour at lunch-time so that staff, if they wish, can socialise;
- extend the rest area, so that staff can sit and chat if they wish, rather than sitting at their own desks during breaks.

These changes are introduced immediately, and within a month everyone reports vast improvements. In order that the morale does not drop so low again in future, the board of directors has introduced a suggestion box for staff ideas. Also, weekly staff meetings with open agendas are now a regular feature of life at 3R.

JOB SATISFACTION

Employees look for:

- Challenging and interesting work
- Opportunities to learn new skills
- Agreeable work environment

- Recognition through promotion and in-service training courses
- An adequate salary and fringe benefits
- Responsibilities
- A word of thanks now and again, it costs little but means a lot

Everyone, both employers and employees sometimes asks themselves the question, 'Is this the right job for me?'. If an employee feels dissatisfied in work, he or she should ask himself or herself the following questions about what it is he or she wants:

- More money?
- Longer holiday allowance?
- Better contractual terms?
- More recognition for efforts?
- More time for outside interests?
- An office or a bigger office?
- A personal assistant?
- More challenging tasks?
- More responsibility?
- More variety of work?
- An expense account?
- Less travelling?
- Better refreshments?

It may be that a current job cannot provide more money or more challenging tasks. But the task of analysing and focusing on individual needs is central to an understanding of yourself and your values.

ANALYSE NEEDS

To be an effective manager it is important to understand that job satisfaction requires change. What might be a stimulating activity one year, may become a boring duty the next. In the mid 1950s, Maslow, a pioneer in management psychology, put forward the theory that there are five basic needs which people aim to satisfy:

1 Physiological need: food, clothing, shelter.
2 Safety need: the need for security.
3 Social need: the need to belong and feel accepted in a social situation.
4 Esteem need: the need to have status and respect from other people.
5 Self-fulfilment need: the need to feel fulfilled through the creative use of one's natural aptitudes.

MAJOR FACTORS WHICH INFLUENCE JOB SATISFACTION

Here again, it is important to remember the wide range of personalities which make up an organisation. Although it could probably be agreed that extra unpaid hours would increase everyone's dissatisfaction, the effect of other factors may vary a lot between individuals. Take a training course on report writing, for example: employees who have been happily writing reports for years might resent being expected to attend a course on a subject they feel quite expert at already. In contrast, a new employee who is eager to learn and ambitious for rapid promotion might regard any extra training as a step up the ladder to a better, higher paid job.

What is important is that assumptions are not made by management alone about what increases job satisfaction and motivation. It is vital that staff are encouraged to make suggestions and provide feedback on management incentives and schemes, in order that a true assessment of job satisfaction can be made. Also, it is important to have regard for the range of different personalities which make up the workforce, and to take into account the differences in employees' expectations and experiences.

Because of the great human variety in an organisation it would be impossible to draw up a list of all the factors which influence job satisfaction or dissatisfaction. Generally speaking you will find that boring and repetitive jobs are least likely to stimulate employees. However, you might discover that many people in these jobs work hard and for long hours, because they are trying to earn enough money to enjoy the other part of their lives; their leisure time. Different types of reward are appropriate in different situations, although it must be recognised that for many people work is a reward in itself. Listed below are general factors which play a part in influencing the world of work.

Job satisfaction may be increased through:

- Being valued and stretched to make the most of your potential
- Supportive management
- Workplace facilities such as canteens, crèches, after-school clubs, holiday playschemes
- Working as part of a team
- Pay and other rewards
- Availability of training
- Relationships with colleagues and boss
- Healthy working environment
- Opportunities to learn and try out new ideas
- Good promotion prospects
- Worthwhile job
- Perks and benefits
- Regular staff appraisals
- Variety in the working day

E X E R C I S E

Place the points listed above in the order in which, from the highest to the lowest, you would be influenced by them in a job. Compare the results amongst the rest of the group. What are the most common factors mentioned by the group which influence job satisfaction?

Of course, there are several other influencing factors. An employee with a keen and time-consuming hobby outside work might value flexitime far more than extra pay, whereas a recent house buyer might well prefer the extra money to help with the mortgage. So, as an individual's needs change and are influenced by other pressures outside the working environment, his or her satisfaction with particular working conditions also change.

MAJOR FACTORS WHICH INFLUENCE JOB DISSATISFACTION

- Stress caused by overwork or underwork
- No flexibility
- Poor morale in the workforce
- Repetitive or monotonous work
- Overstrict management
- Dangerous or unhealthy working environment
- Discrimination because of being female or a minority ethnic worker or due to a disability
- Sexual harassment
- Passed over for a pay rise that was deserved
- Overlooked for promotion
- Low pay
- Few perks or incentives
- Little recognition from management
- Too much unhelpful interference from management

EXERCISE

First design an appropriate questionnaire. Using your questionnaire, do a survey of local people to discover what they find to be the most and least rewarding/satisfying aspects of their work.

Another complaint often heard amongst professional people and those with several formal qualifications is that they are no longer doing the job they have been trained to do. The higher up the ladder they have climbed, the further away they are from the original skills and knowledge they acquired during professional training. Too much time is spent on administrative jobs and supervision, rather than on the client group with whom they had initially wanted to work. This problem is very common in people-oriented jobs such as the careers service, social services, personnel, and professional human resource jobs. Quite often the price paid for promotion is a high one, with a move away from face-to-face contact with people, to be swamped under a mountain of paper work and planning tasks. So, on the one hand, although many people would welcome promotion and feel certain that it would increase job satisfaction, in reality the reverse can also happen.

There can be little doubt that job satisfaction has a major influence on a whole range of workplace processes and employee relations. Put simply, a happy employee is more likely to do a good job than one who is dissatisfied with his or her job. A person who is valued is more likely to value the organisation than one who feels undervalued. Similarly a person who feels that his career development and progress is being taken seriously is more likely to remain loyal and stay with the organisation than one who feels that his development is being overlooked or ignored.

In terms of an organisation keen to succeed and develop good employee relations, the features of effective people management are outlined below.

Job satisfaction	Job dissatisfaction
• good attendance	• high absence rate
• high morale	• low morale
• increased motivation	• reduced motivation
• better cooperation	• low cooperation
• greater productivity	• lower productivity
• low staff turnover	• high staff turnover
• good company image	• bad company image

So it is clear that the higher the number of employees who experience job satisfaction, the better the chance of higher productivity and company success. It could be argued that in the current climate of increased competition within a single European market, job satisfaction is an essential ingredient for ensuring the continued success of each company.

METHODS OF IMPROVING MORALE

Job satisfaction and workplace morale contribute towards company success or failure. Evidence shows that an organisation's most valuable asset is its people: the employees who put a company's aims and objectives into practice daily.

Businesses which put people first and treat staff's requirements as a high priority stand a much greater chance of success than those which take employees for granted. 'People friendly' workplaces have a higher chance of keeping their staff than those that are not. At a time when the working population is ageing and employees are being wooed by the prospect of working in other EC countries, it is essential that job satisfaction should be high on the employers' agenda.

Improving morale and providing job satisfaction for the whole workforce cannot be left to chance. Relying on chance alone will not guarantee a contented workforce, neither will it guarantee a profitable turnover. Improving workplace morale is like any other business activity: it requires careful planning in order to get the best results.

EXERCISE

All groups, whether in a working environment or a college environment are really just miniature versions of the larger environment called society. Think of the morale in your group at the moment; would you describe it as high or low? Discuss and draw up a list of as many ways as possible to improve workplace morale. What do you think would be the benefits of an improvement in morale among the group?

In order to improve morale it is first necessary to increase motivation. Motivation comes from the word 'motive': an inducement or incentive. Imagine getting an offer of a fabulous job which you are convinced you would really enjoy. One of the criteria involved in getting the job is to pass a certain number of exams or get certain grades. Suddenly, the motivation or desire to pass the exams is increased. Motivation increases when employees see a point in what they are doing and are valued for doing it.

Methods of improving work morale and, in the long run, performance and productivity are known as motivators. Again, what motivates one person to arrive early, work hard, increase his or her output, might differ greatly from what motivates another. In general though, it is possible to identify a number of common factors which 'drive' people.

MOTIVATORS

- The work itself
- Achievement: a sense of achievement and success
- Recognition: for your achievements
- Responsibility
- Status
- Career development
- Financial rewards

Behind each of these motivators is one underlying factor: a supportive environment and an effective management team. After all, many people would regard extra responsibility, for instance, as a threat and find the added burden very stressful. However, with management's support and encouragement, an employee's overall sense of achievement is likely to increase.

HERZBERG'S TWIN FACTOR THEORY: MOTIVATORS AND HYGIENE FACTORS

Researchers have demonstrated that whether consciously or unconsciously, workers do have other factors in mind as necessary components of job satisfaction. One American management specialist, Frederick Herzberg, published in the mid 1960s a paper which stated that there are two sets of factors related to job satisfaction and the lack of it. Based on a large number of interviews, Herzberg was able to draw up a table which identified the major satisfiers as:

- Achievement in the job
- Recognition for doing a good job
- Satisfaction deriving from the work itself
- Being given responsibility for an area of work
- Receiving advancement at work

The factors identified as dissatisfiers were:

- Dissatisfaction with company policy
- Supervision and technical conditions
- Salary rate

- Interpersonal relationships with colleagues
- Working conditions

Herzberg related the satisfiers to the job the employee does and the dissatisfiers with the environment. His thesis was that the presence of the former would provide a source of motivation, while the presence of the latter – excellent pay, great colleagues and a superb office – while avoiding job dissatisfaction would not in themselves motivate and were therefore only 'hygiene factors' or, as we might say today, 'cosmetic factors'. For instance, a manager who receives a brilliant pay rise and a new office might work that much harder for a couple of weeks, but will soon become accustomed to his or her higher living standards and revert to former work patterns.

Companies which are people-friendly and not just product-friendly have a higher chance of market success than others. All too often in the past, an employee's input and output has been measured solely in terms of his or her nine to five shift, and little account has been taken of the person 'beyond' the job. As a result, any outside influence, such as family needs, friends, running a home, have been regarded as having no effect on job performance whatsoever. Nowadays however, many firms are recognising that what an employee's life outside work is like has a direct impact on job performance. This is only common sense, since few of us can switch between work and home roles easily. In the past, a common complaint from women returning to work after having a baby, has been to find that their employers behave as if nothing has happened. This can only serve to increase stress and reduce job satisfaction. Fortunately, more organisations are developing the supportive environment which effective management of human resources recognises as the key factor towards overall success.

EXERCISE

Draw up a checklist of the factors which ought to be taken into account to ensure that the maximum number of employees experience greater job satisfaction than dissatisfaction.

QUALITY CIRCLES (QCs)

Since the late 1970s the use of quality circles has shot up. QC work mainly originated within companies in the production sector, especially major car manufacturers. A typical quality circle consists of a group of between five and eight volunteers from the same workplace. The circle meet for an hour or so each week under the guidance of a supervisor to solve work-related problems in their departments.

It is widely felt that participating in quality circles helps encourage employees to accept responsibility, identify with company aims and participate in company life. In general, this helps to foster cooperation and improve the working climate. The circle's members may freely discuss the difficulties in their line of work, thereby helping to sort out any necessary changes and agree solutions. There are many advantages of quality circles, including:

- an increase in employee's production performance, since quality circles help focus on work and methods of improving output;
- helping to highlight progress, which in turn helps the circle's members to identify their strengths and weaknesses and make further progress;
- if employees feel that their ideas are falling on fertile soil, their perception of their own value and worth is strengthened;
- greater involvement in company life brought about by quality circles leads to greater motivation, which results in greater productivity.

A well-motivated workforce and high morale should by itself reduce staff turnover. Staff are less likely to leave if they are happy, fulfilled, feel valued, and if there is a good working atmosphere. The increased competition of the single European market will persuade companies to make better use of their human resources. No employer with an eye on success wants to lose trained staff, since management wants a return on its investment in training.

E XERCISE

Choose two people you know who are in work. If possible, find one person who has stayed with the same company for a long time and another who has had a variety of jobs. Find out what made the first person stay with the one company and what influenced the second person to change jobs frequently.

Of course, many influences outside work determine whether a person will remain in a job. In an economic recession, only the very brave or highly skilled can afford to jump in and out of jobs. For most people, the facts of life such as mortgages, dependants and children's schooling play a major role in their working life and determine how free or not they are to leave their job.

Again, every employee should be encouraged and supported in his or her career. In the past, very rigid work hierarchies and inflexible decision making processes have caused staff to lose sight of how everything slots together in an organisation. The result is that employees often find it more worthwhile to express their creative potential and ideas exclusively within the private sphere (i.e. working to live). All too often this has resulted in increased staff turnover, as individuals leave to find more interesting work. However, a greater number of businesses are now recognising the impact of flexibility in two ways:

1 Flexible working arrangements, for example, flexitime, term-time contracts, homeworking.
2 Flexibility in management attitudes, as opposed to rigid one-sided control of employees by employers. The trend towards increased flexibility in many companies has produced far higher workplace morale which in turn has reduced staff turnover.

PUTTING POLICY INTO PRACTICE

A policy on human resource management is an important tool to ensure that all good intentions made are put into practice. However, even the best policy is likely to have little or no effect unless it is accompanied by a programme of activities.

Clearly, workplace policies vary between organisations and what may be a very useful exercise in a large business might be of little use in a smaller organisation. A business which employs thousands of people is more likely to have a well-staffed personnel department than a small business. However, as with equal opportunities, policies and decision making should not be seen as the exclusive job of personnel departments. When this is the case the policy tends to be treated as a separate issue which has nothing to do with the majority of the workforce. The main purpose of any policy is that it benefits all the workforce and not only those that create it.

EXERCISE

What local organisations could a small company contact for advice and information on planning and implementing a workplace policy on human resource management? Draw up a checklist of useful sources of information.

Whatever the size or nature of an organisation, the following five steps should be taken when implementing a good policy.

1 Planning

How? Why? When? are the three questions at the centre of any planning task. A team of personnel from as wide a cross section of the workforce as possible should be involved in the planning stage. It is the team's responsibility to meet regularly and decide upon priorities. To ensure that policy actually becomes practice, the activities and goals should be planned within set time periods. Without this there is a danger that ideas remain as just ideas far longer than they need to.

Some of the issues which the team could address might include:

- Canteen facilities: how could they be improved? Do they provide employees with a healthy, well-balanced menu?
- Workplace childcare policy: are we doing enough to enable employees to combine effectively their roles as employees and parents?
- Equal opportunities: are we putting our policy into practice?

2 Aims and objectives

What do we want to achieve and how best may we achieve it? Goal setting within realistic time spans is the ideal way to bring about improvements.

3 Decision making

Ideally, when a strategy has been planned, decisions as to how it should be implemented ought to be decided jointly between management and employees. Participation in decision making helps to ensure that an activity is not only relevant and appropriate, but that it reflects the wishes of the majority of the workforce.

4 Activities

Well-thought out and well-timed activities are the practical element of any workplace policy. They are also one of the most important elements, and should never be overlooked. Activities are a direct measure of the policy's success and show what effect it is having in practice. Whichever business activities are chosen they should aim to benefit all the workforce, and not merely those staff who selected them.

5 Review

In order to check that the policy is actually working and having the desired effect, it needs to be reviewed regularly and any changes or improvements made. Also, a review enables new ideas and suggestions to be incorporated into the policy, so that it does not become stale and out of date. Obviously workplaces change, both in the make up of the workforce as new people join and others leave, and also in their business activities. A regular assessment of the policy through a review ensures that it is always relevant and up to date.

EMPLOYEE PARTICIPATION IN DECISION MAKING

If all decision making is in the hands of management then it runs the risk of bearing very little resemblance to reality. For example, if a decision about the noise level on the shopfloor is made by the company director from his or her top-floor suite, then it is not made from a position of knowledge or experience. It is very important, therefore, that everyone is consulted and whenever possible participates in decision making. After all, business is all about relationships between people. At the heart of decision making lie the formal and informal channels of communication. An increase in good policy and practice is really an ode to communication: business and communication are the two links of a single chain and to break one is to break the other.

The benefits to organisations of employee participation in decision making include:

- employees are more likely to accept responsibility for new ideas, or methods and procedures which they had a part in forming;
- an increase in commitment, which often leads to an increase in productivity;
- an increase in loyalty to the company;
- fostering cooperation between colleagues;
- improving the working climate and staff morale;
- joint decisions in which employees have an equal say are more likely to be a true reflection of needs, than decisions made entirely by management;
- an increase in self-worth and feeling of being valued;
- contributing to the company is likely to increase job satisfaction;

Above all, decisions which are made jointly ensure that they are relevant and appropriate, and not merely a paper exercise.

EXERCISE

Make a checklist of the benefits which can be derived from joint decision making. Ask people you know who are in employment; do they have much say in what goes on at work, or are rules and regulations and new working procedures always imposed without consultation?

One of the major benefits of increased participation is that employees are able to express their creative potential in the workplace, if ideas are made welcome and fall on fertile soil. It should be remembered that everyone has a creative potential that is infinitely greater than the potential he or she actually uses. This potential can be released by encouraging as much participation as possible in all decision making at all levels within an organisation. The earlier such participation is encouraged the more effective all policy measures will be, and this may well be the best way to avoid the bad effects of the NIH (not invented here) syndrome. Experience shows that even the most ridiculous idea enables an organisation to detect a positive note, which in turn leads to greater commitment to policy developments.

E X E R C I S E

Decisions are often made either formally, for example in meetings or conferences, or informally, in the canteen, in the corridor, or during a conversation between colleagues. What methods might an organisation introduce to improve its channels of communication?

Again it is important to emphasise the differences which exist between the different people which make up an organisation. Not only are there the obvious differences such as male and female, old and young, disabled and able-bodied, black and white but also the more subtle differences in the personalities and characters which work together. While some people may welcome a chance to participate in workplace decisions, others may be quite unwilling to do so and feel threatened by the prospect. If, for example, an employee has worked for a company for years and has never been asked to contribute an opinion or make a suggestion for improvements, he or she might feel quite afraid at suddenly being expected to do so. Suggestion boxes have an important part to play. A suggestion box is an indirect way of inviting employees to contribute their thoughts about an issue, without being confronted directly. In very large organisations it would be virtually impossible to ask everyone individually for their opinion. Not only would it be extremely time consuming but it would also be likely to turn into an enormous administration task and very little would be achieved. Suggestion boxes are one way of ensuring that at least everyone gets the opportunity to influence what is, after all, their workplace.

E X E R C I S E

Write a report entitled 'Methods of encouraging staff participation in decision making'. For ideas, ask a range of people you know who are in employment, how their companies encourage staff to participate in company life.

10

WELFARE AT WORK

If we are to believe that an organisation's most important asset is its people then the welfare of staff must come high on the business agenda. The days when a small group of managers could control their employees by rules and regulations which had little regard for joint decision making have become a thing of the past. Today, much more emphasis is placed on cooperation and good relations between managers and employees. The advantages of this include:

- a much higher level of mutual trust which in turn leads to increased respect;
- a better working environment which by itself helps to increase productivity, which in turn increases a company's chance of success;
- an increase in company loyalty which helps to reduce staff turnover, and reduce the costs associated with recruitment and selection

WELFARE PROVISION

In the past, employee welfare was regarded solely as the preserve of the trade unions rather than employers. Trade unions had their eye mainly on increasing the rewards for the employees, while managers were more concerned with profit and productivity. The last decade has seen a new working relationship develop between managers and unions. Staff welfare has become a major element of human resource management.

Clearly the needs of a large organisation which employs many thousands of people are very different from a small business. The one factor they do have in common however, and which they both rely on equally for success, is their communication network. Whatever welfare systems are introduced, it is essential that they fill a real need and are not merely imposed on staff from a management point of view. The success of a welfare service lies in its acceptance by the workforce, and that can only be measured by its take-up rate. An in-house jacuzzi and squash court might look absolutely marvellous, but if it is not what staff want, nor what they are likely to use regularly, then it is of very little benefit.

The most reliable method of assessing what the most appropriate type of welfare is likely to be, is to ask staff for their opinions. In a large business this can be done by distributing questionnaires, providing suggestion boxes and holding departmental meetings. The whole process of assessing what is needed might take a couple of weeks or even months to get a clear and accurate picture. In a small organisation, daily contact between the entire workforce is much more likely, so that it is easier to arrive at an informal system of reaching agreement on popular welfare choices.

EXERCISE

You are the personnel manager of a large firm with a workforce of 2000. Produce a questionnaire for distribution among all departments entitled 'Your welfare at work – how can we help?'.

THE LARGE BUSINESS

Large organisations are well equipped to provide staff with a whole range of welfare services. The services made available are to the benefit of both employers and employees, and should not be seen as an expensive and time-consuming extra. Many companies in the UK now provide health care services. This makes sense for both parties since a healthy workforce:

- has a lower rate of absenteeism due to sickness (in 1991 the number of days lost through sickness reached 500 million for the first time since records have been kept. More than a third of absences were through stress-related illnesses);
- is better able to work more effectively, which in turn will increase productivity and company success.

A wide range of health services have been developed within the world of work in recent years. Listed below are some of them.

- Health checks available to all staff over the age of 35
- Health screening
- Breast and cervical screening
- Cancer screening
- Habit-breaker courses for smokers
- Well-women clinics
- Counselling for alcohol related illnesses
- AIDS and HIV counselling

Most of these services are provided free of charge for employees, or subsidised by the employer.

EXERCISE

Find out which large employers in your area provide health services to the workforce. If possible, arrange to visit them or invite a guest speaker to your group. Find out what services are available and what the take-up rate is among the workforce.

An increasing number of employers are mentioning welfare services in their job advertisements to attract good staff. Look through national and local newspapers and make a list of those companies which are doing so.

SMALL AND MEDIUM-SIZED ENTERPRISES

There would be little point in an organisation which employs relatively few staff to provide an in-house gym or company canteen. But although the services made available for staff welfare may be on a less grand scale than those offered at the multinational company down the road, they are still of central importance to the wellbeing of the staff and company as a whole.

D ISCUSSION POINT

What might a small company introduce to ensure that staff welfare is taken seriously? Small and medium-sized companies could twin with other local companies and introduce services such as cancer screening, or habit-breaking courses by bringing in outside experts for training and counselling sessions. What else might a small employer consider?

DIFFERENT TYPES OF WELFARE PROVISION

CANTEENS

Several large employers in the UK have staff canteens. In fact, many have two types: a canteen for the workforce and a management restaurant. Many employers subsidise the cost of running a canteen so that employees can eat the main meal of the day for considerably less than the usual price. Canteens also have a social function, and enable staff to meet informally in the workplace.

CHILDCARE SERVICES

A growing number of employers are providing some form of childcare services. The most common are:

- workplace crèches and nurseries;
- after-school playschemes;
- time off for child sickness;
- childcare cheques which are redeemable by childminders;
- childcare links: employers contribute to a childcare information and referral service;
- holiday playschemes;
- childcare vouchers have been introduced by Luncheon Vouchers and can only be exchanged for childcare.

One reason for the increase in the provision of childcare amenities is that demographic changes in the labour market mean that companies will need to attract more women with childcare responsibilities back to work during the 1990s. There are several ways of doing this:

Flexible working: by allowing staff to work flexitime, an organisation enables them to combine childcare with work.

Job sharing: a job share is simply a job done by two people. Normally the hours are divided in half, either mornings and afternoons or half a week each.

The benefits to employers of jobsharing:

- a lower turnover of staff;
- additional cover in peak periods;
- greater flexibility;
- better continuity, due to less absence for domestic reasons and halving the impact of absence for sickness;
- a wider range of skills, sharers can contribute different skills;
- a wider employment pool which includes those who cannot work full-time;
- jobsharers' outside interests may bring new approachs and knowledge to the job;
- the skills of those not able to work full-time are retained

Term-time only contract: allows parents with school-age children to work full-time but only during school terms.

Career break schemes: women who take maternity leave may return to their job or one at the same level at any time within the limits of the career break (usually between three to five years).

Childcare assistance: this method varies, it includes the provision of a workplace nursery, a playscheme for school holidays, or a financial contribution towards childcare costs.

Working from home: many of the hi-tech companies, such as International Computers Ltd (ICL), have fitted computers in their employees' homes. The company employs hundreds of women on flexible-hours contracts, many of them return to full-time work on site after a few years.

There are many advantages to employers of providing childcare help:

- recruitment: childcare and parent-friendly working policies and practices attract staff;
- retention: women are more likely to return to work after maternity leave if childcare is provided;
- equal opportunities: assistance with childcare encourages equality of access to all employment opportunities for all staff;
- company image: flexible working practices and help with childcare are essential for a modern company;
- cost effectiveness: the Midland Bank estimates that they lose £17,000 in recruitment, training and management costs for every employee who does not return after maternity leave. In response, they have now embarked on a programme of 300 nurseries for staff, and find their average subsidy of £1,700 per child per year produces real value for money.

FREE TRANSPORT TO WORK

Many companies run a coach or minibus service to and from the workplace. This is cost effective when large numbers of people live in the same area. It is also, of course, environmentally-friendly since it cuts down considerably on the number of vehicles on the road.

CLOTHING ALLOWANCE

For businesses where staff uniforms are required, many employers provide an allowance towards the cost or provide the clothing itself. In other industries, where the type of dress to be worn is laid down by management, an allowance or bonus is included in the salary to cover the costs of the work clothes.

TRADE UNION ACTIVITY

Trade unions grew out of the industrial revolution and were formed by and for workers to protect their jobs and their wages. Today they are involved in much more than job protection, tackling such wide-ranging issues as sexual harassment, disciplinary and grievance cases, pay settlements, childcare, maternity and paternity rights, and equal opportunities policies and practices. In addition, many unions also run training and educational courses for their members to help them keep up to date on changes in the law and keep ahead in educational developments.

EXERCISE

Write down the name of four major trade unions in the UK. Contact one of them to find out what their membership rate is. Also, ask people you know who are in employment and find out how many of them belong to a trade union. As well as its involvement in pay negotiations and employment disputes, does their union provide any welfare services for members?

PROTECTING THE RIGHTS OF EMPLOYEES

A union will ensure that employers provide a clearly defined and fair contract of employment covering issues such as hours of work, holiday entitlements, overtime or bonus payments, pensions and maternity/paternity leave. It will also ensure that working conditions are safe and legal, for example, that an organisation has adequate washroom and sanitary facilities, protection against hazardous material and sufficient breaks for VDU users

Providing the union is recognised by the employers, it will negotiate the best pay deal through formal bargaining procedures. It can also advise on rights: redundancy, maternity leave, right to time off for family responsibilities and the rights of part-time employees and, in the event of unfair dismissal, sex discrimination or equal pay complaints, a union will take up a case with management.

Finally, a union will also represent members in court if settlements out of court cannot be reached. In 1990 the TGWU won over 60 million pounds in compensation awards for members.

IMPROVING WORKING CONDITIONS

A union can take up complaints or grievances against employers if working conditions are poor and can negotiate better deals than the statutory minimum, for example, redundancy and maternity packages, part-time worker entitlements, and bonus scheme rewards. Unions also work with employers to draw up special agreements, for example, a policy on sexual harassment, health and safety, and exert pressure on employers to provide welfare services and childcare facilities.

OTHER BENEFITS

Most unions now have women's officers or equality officers to ensure that women's issues receive high priority, and breast and cervical screening programmes have been set up in some workplaces as a result of requests to management by a union. Unions have succeeded in negotiating improvements in pension schemes and there are also many other financial benefits: sickness, accident, unemployment and 'dispute' benefits, as well as convalescent homes or hotels (free or subsidised) for recovery from illness. Free educational and training courses, competitively priced car and house insurance, mortgages, loans and other discounts, for example, on holidays and travel costs.

EMPLOYERS' ASSOCIATIONS

In the same way as employees join together to form trade unions in order to protect their rights, employers form employers' associations. There are now some 400 employers' associations in the UK. Each association is different, but there are some features common to all of them.

The majority of associations are open to all employers in a particular industry and aim to cover as many of them as possible in all geographical areas. Most employers' associations are funded entirely by members subscriptions.

Structure in employers' associations varies greatly, but there are two main types of structure common in the UK. Some organisations are single national groups which aim to recruit all the organisations in their industry directly. They may have branches operating in local areas. Other associations recruit locally and have a national body to which all the associations belong. An example of this type is the Engineering Employers' Federation and its local associations.

Staffing also varies. Some employ a large number of full or part-time staff specialising in all kinds of subjects. Others have no permanent staff at all and rely on local members as central figures to recruit new members and publicise the association.

Much of the work of employers' associations is to provide information and advice to members on such subjects as the law and commerce. Some associations are active in employee relations and negotiations with trade unions. Sometimes too, the larger associations will become involved in assisting with employee disputes which cannot be handled within the member company.

DISCUSSION POINT

Employers' associations like trade unions have declined in membership since the end of the Second World War. What reasons can you think of for this fall in numbers?

ENGINEERING EMPLOYERS' FEDERATION (EEF)

The Engineers Employers' Federation is one of the largest employers' federations in the UK. It has over 15 local associations which cover the whole of the UK and together constitute the Engineering Employers' Federation. Each association is concerned with providing a service and representing the interests of the engineering industry on all aspects of employment and industrial relations, including:

- Trade union negotiations
- Avoidance and settlements of disputes
- Industrial law
- Wages and working conditions
- Advice on labour market conditions
- Contact with government and other official bodies and committees
- Health and safety
- Training
- Research and development

Any engineering company, whatever its size may join the EEF. Member firms range in size from the smallest with only one employee to the largest with approximately 14,000.

THE TRADES UNION CONGRESS (TUC) AND THE CONFEDERATION OF BRITISH INDUSTRY (CBI)

The TUC is the umbrella body to which trade unions belong or 'affiliate'. Some trade unions are, however, independent of the TUC, for example, the Society of Authors. The TUC is matched by the employers' CBI: the Confederation of British Industry.

The CBI represents over 10,000 members and speaks on behalf of all employers' organisations. Its main role is to represent employers' organisations to the rest of the country and to the government in particular.

HEALTH AND SAFETY LEGISLATION

The main law covering health and safety in the workplace is the Health and Safety at Work Act 1974 (HASAWA). This law protects everyone affected by working activities; not only immediate employees but students, trainees, contractors, passers-by and casual visitors too. The employer must provide a safe and healthy workplace with appropriate welfare services.

DISCUSSION POINT

Think about the building you are in at the moment. What kind of health and safety measures does it have to safeguard the wellbeing of the people who use it regularly? Do you think it is enough or could more be done to ensure maximum safety?

The law states that an employer must make sure that:

- employees are not exposed to risks to their health as a result of using, handling, transporting or storing products and substances;
- employees must be provided with information and training and the supervision necessary to ensure health and safety;
- safe systems of work are set and followed;
- the workplace has safe entry and exit routes;
- employees have adequate working conditions including adequate lighting, heating, ventilation and toilet facilities;
- all firms employing five or more staff must prepare a written health and safety policy. Smaller firms also require a policy to ensure that they are meeting their obligations under HASAWA;
- all workplaces should have an accident book to record injuries, diseases and deaths. Under the Reporting of Injuries, Diseases and Dangerous Occurrences Regulations 1985 (RIDDOR) an employer must notify the Health and Safety Executive (HSE) or local authority of any accident which results in the death or severe injury to a person, or which causes incapacity for more than three days. Also, any 'notifiable dangerous occurence' must be reported. This might include:
  - overloading of an electrical circuit;
  - the collapse of load-bearing equipment such as cranes;
  - an explosion or fire;
  - the release of flammable liquid;
  - dust, fume and noise levels which are out of control;
- first-aid and the reporting of injuries sustained at work applies to all employers whatever their size or nature. The Health and Safety (first aid) Regulations 1981 state that an employer must provide first-aid equipment, facilities and personnel, and inform all employees of the arrangements for first-aid.

Health and safety at work is an important issue which should not be ignored, and ignorance of the law and the obligations it places upon employers provides no excuse. Accidents at work can mean extra costs and damaged machinery, not to mention ruined lives. Small workplaces have worse accident records than large ones. Around 400,000 people are injured at work every year, some 12,000 of them seriously. About 500 people are killed. In addition to these figures, taken from publication number 16 of the HSE, *The Law on Health and Safety at Work*, there is an even higher number of employees who develop work-related diseases such as deafness, Repetitive Strain Injury (RSI), heart disease, bronchitis, dermatitis and cancer.

Several good employers have gone beyond the minimum standards laid down by the law to ensure that their workforce is well looked after, and exposed to the minimum amount of risk. Local health and safety inspectors can advise businesses on how to draw up a health and safety policy statement. They may also help to train safety representatives who are appointed by trade unions.

Listed below are some factors a company might consider:

- Are the toilet and rest facilities adequate?
- Are there enough non-smoking areas provided?
- Are the canteen menus adequate ?
- Is the protective clothing and equipment adequate, up to date and always used in the correct manner?
- Is the workplace clean?
- Is the ventilation and lighting adequate?
- Are the firedoors and exits always kept clear and new staff or visitors always made aware of their whereabouts?

EXERCISE

With the group, arrange to visit a variety of businesses, such as a local factory, warehouse, large retailer, or public building such as the local library, swimming baths or law courts. Find out what each has done to maintain adequate health and safety standards in the workplace. Are posters displayed in several places? Are staff aware of their rights under the health and safety laws and have they got a workplace health and safety representative? Write a report on your findings and present it to the group.

If you cannot arrange actually to visit a workplace, ask someone you know who is in employment, about the health and safety 'ethos' of their workplace. You might find it helpful to ask questions such as :

- Do they know what their rights are under the law?
- Do they know who is in charge of first aid in their workplace?
- Would they know how to go about reporting an accident?
- Are there any HMSO posters or leaflets on health and safety in their workplace?
- Have they received any formal health and safety training?

The answers you receive should help you assess how seriously or otherwise health and safety issues are regarded in the world of work. What else do you consider ought to be done in employment to promote the health, safety and welfare of staff?

CONTROL OF SUBSTANCES HAZARDOUS TO HEALTH (COSHH) REGULATIONS 1988

The COSHH regulations cover substances including gases, chemicals, vapours, dust, viruses and bacteria. Under COSHH laws employers have a number of legal obligations. These include:

- assessment of risk in the workplace. The assessment must be carried out by a competent person and cover the substances used in the workplace, as well as the transport, storage or disposal methods of these substances. It must also include a breakdown of the possible health hazards associated with each substance, and a review of the current health and safety precautions;
- monitoring exposure and health surveillance;
- prevention and control of exposure;

- information, instruction and training;
- written records must be kept of the assessments which are done; environmental monitoring for five years, and employees' health surveillance for 30 years

EXERCISE

Divide your group into two subgroups, called A and B.

Group A Task: research either the HASAWA or the COSSH regulations. Write a summary of the major features for distribution among your group.

Group B task: arrange to visit a couple of local employers. Try to speak to a representative from management and one from the union. What impact have the COSSH regulations, introduced in 1988, had on the workplace?

ENFORCEMENT RESPONSIBILITIES

The Health and Safety Commission was set up to monitor the HASAWA. It oversees the HSE. Health and safety inspectors may visit any workplace without giving prior notice, although an employer may ask to see proof of identification. Under the HASAWA, responsibility for enforcing the health and safety regulations in certain types of workplaces is transferred from the HSE to local authorities. The types of businesses that local authority environmental health officers are responsible for include:

- Retailing
- Office work
- Catering services
- Various leisure activities
- Care or treatment of animals
- Caravan and campsites
- Tyre and exhaust fitting services in garages

The HSE factory inspectors are in charge of factory workplaces, agricultural businesses, construction, local authorities, police, fire authorities and crown premises.

REGISTERING THE WORKPLACE

All workplaces must be registered with the appropriate enforcement authority. In general, employers in factories and manufacturing workshops should register with the HSE. Employers in shops, offices, warehouses, catering and leisure services should register with the local council by contacting the environmental health department.

OTHER HEALTH AND SAFETY REGULATIONS

EMPLOYERS' LIABILITY (COMPULSORY INSURANCE) ACT 1969

This obliges all employers in the UK to be insured against liability for injury or disease in the course of employment. Evidence of liability insurance must be displayed so that it may be easily seen and read by all employees and visitors.

FIRE CERTIFICATE

Almost all employers need a fire certificate. The local fire authority can make an exemption for a business where the fire risk is very low, but you cannot be exempted unless you apply, so it is worth contacting the authority for advice.

OFFICIAL HEALTH AND SAFETY POSTERS

Under the Health and Safety Information for Employees Regulations 1989, all employers must display an official poster or distribute an official leaflet to all employees. These posters and leaflets are available from HMSO.

EUROPEAN COMMUNITY LAW

Health policy is principally a national concern, but like most laws, new regulations are constantly being generated by the European Commission in Brussels. Concern about health protection and disease prevention are of practical importance to the ageing European population, and to employers in maintaining a high standard of staff welfare. The EC has been involved in public awareness campaigns and health research for many years. The 'European year of safety, hygiene and health protection at work' in 1992 has paved the way for an increase in good practice.

There are a number of EC Directives which lay down specific requirements in relation to health and safety which apply to the UK, and all other EC member states. Proposals to update the law on basic health, safety and welfare requirements in the workplace in order to bring UK law in line with EC law have been put forward by the Health and Safety Commission. These will fulfil the requirements of the European Directive on minimum standards and health requirements for the workplaces (the so called 'Workplace Directive').

The proposed changes to the law will cover the great majority of workplaces, whereas most current British law is limited mainly to factories, offices and shops. Schools, for example, will in future also be covered. The new regulations cover:

- General health and safety management
- Work equipment safety
- Manual handling of loads
- Workplace conditions (health, safety and welfare)
- Personal protective equipment
- Display screen equipment

A number of HSE publications giving guidance on the new regulations and approved codes of practice are available from the HSE. A good deal of practical guidance on the new regulations is available from the Health and Safety Commission, and from environmental health departments in local authorities.

OTHER WELFARE ISSUES

COMPANY MAGAZINES

In a large company a magazine is an ideal way of ensuring that everything of importance is communicated to the whole workforce. A magazine's editorial team should be drawn from as wide a cross-section of the company as possible so that as many views as possible are included. Company magazines fulfill several functions, including:

- everyone keeps up to date on important changes, both internal changes such as company policy and external ones such as changes in national laws such as health and safety regulations;
- provides a means of communication and ensures that everyone has the opportunity to participate in company life;
- involves all departments working together more closely than in day-to-day company life;
- enables organisations such as banks and major high street retail chain stores which have branches all over the country, to communicate with each other, and increases the feeling of belonging to the company;
- for multi-site businesses such as banks, building societies and high street retailers it enables good ideas and examples of good practice to be exchanged nationally. An increase in good practice is the best way to ensure overall company success.

EXERCISE

Think of an organisation to which you belong, or have in the past, a school or youth club, for example; did it have an internal magazine or newsletter? If so, what sort of information did it contain? What other advantages are there of this form of communication?

Magazine content obviously varies between organisations. It is up to the editorial team to decide what is important to include. Whatever the contents, a magazine should attempt to reflect the interests of as broad a cross-section of the workforce as possible. Some ideas for a magazine's editorial team to consider are:

- sales and company product details and prices, with information on forthcoming products and their launch dates;
- a page entitled, 'What does this department do?', is relevant for large companies with several departments so that each department is aware of what is going on. The 'department' page may be changed every month, or however often the magazine is published;
- a diary of staff social events;
- a sports page;
- a suggestion page for staff to express any new ideas;
- company competitions and external events about which staff might wish to know;

- in-house training courses;
- an achievements page for the best employee or best department of the month.

PRE-RETIREMENT PLANNING

Considering the fact that the UK workforce is an ageing one, very little attention is paid to the needs of older people approaching retirement. In Chapter 4, we examined equal opportunities issues and age discrimination in employment. Older people face discrimination in employment, and after retirement. One way to prepare older people for retirement is to conduct formal pre-retirement planning.

So far in the UK, only a very small percentage of the workforce receive any form of pre-retirement preparation. The majority of workers are expected to work until the retirement day and then move into retirement with very little support from their former employer or from the state to help them adjust to a new lifestyle. In contrast, young people making the transition from school to employment or training are provided with as much careers and vocational guidance as they require.

There are a number of organisations in the UK which exist to help employers plan and prepare their employees for retirement. They hold pre-retirement courses which address a whole range of issues including:

- Leisure
- Finance and financial planning
- Health and fitness (the health and quality of life in retirement is directly related to the health and quality of life experienced in working years)
- Voluntary work
- Benefits and pension entitlements, as well as reduced costs on public transport and for the use of sports and leisure facilities
- Education

Employers can get help to arrange pre-retirement planning from a number of organisations including Age Concern, the Pre-retirement Association and local TECs. These organisations can give advice and guidance about the re-employment of older workers as trainers of younger workers, and about all the issues associated with making the transition from employment to retirement.

DISCUSSION POINT

What are the advantages of pre-retirement planning from the employee's and employer's points of view? Draw up a list of issues which you consider are important and ought to be included in a pre-retirement programme. Arrange the points in the form of a timetable.

FURTHER READING

Reddy, M. *The manager's guide to counselling at work* British Psychological Society, 1987
Stranks, J. *The manager's guide to health and safety at work* Kogan Page, 1990

REWARDS FOR WORK

One of the most important reasons why people go to work is to earn money. Money is required to buy food, clothes, pay bills and accomodation costs. Different types of jobs have always demanded various pay rewards. Jobs which are deemed to carry little responsibility or only a minimal amount of skill command only low pay, whereas jobs which involve a lot of training or greater responsibility tend to command higher salaries.

EXERCISE

Match the jobs in column A with the salaries in column B and the other elements in column C:

A Job	B Salary	C Reward
Company Director	£160 per week	Long holidays
Joiner	£18,000 per year	Company car
Secretary	£50,000 per year	Free overalls
Van driver	£8,000 per year	Luncheon vouchers
University lecturer	£250 per week	Use of vehicle

PAY

In the world of work, jobs which are traditionally undertaken by women have tended to pay less than jobs which are regarded as men's work. Even today in many industries men's and women's work is divided, with a woman's job having lower status. In many firms, the fact that women have children makes them a liability and often a short-term prospect. Women are often considered unsuitable for certain work, ranging from supervising and managing people to dealing with technical equipment.

All this is, of course, blind prejudice in the face of evidence which shows that women are as efficient and effective as men. However, a company which has not examined its prejudices still acts on them.

DISCUSSION POINT

Arrange a visit to a local engineering company. Find out the numbers of men and women on the shop floor, in the workshop, in the personnel department, and in the administration section. In which jobs are men concentrated, and in which are women concentrated? Find out which jobs are more highly paid.

The Equal Pay Act 1970 was introduced to eliminate discrimination between men and women in pay and other terms of their employment contracts. This includes payments for overtime, bonuses and piecework as well as other conditions of work such as working hours, holidays and sick leave entitlements. The Act applies to people of all ages. It applies equally to full-time, part-time, temporary, contract workers and homeworkers as well as apprentices, self-employed workers and employees. There is no minimum period of employment before an employee can bring an equal pay claim.

RATE OF PAY

The going rate for a job is decided not by the employee but by his or her manager and trade union. Most people probably believe that they are paid too little for the job they do. There is a large degree of personal feelings and opinion involved in deciding why some jobs are paid more or less than others. For example, while some people might agree that working in dangerous or unsanitary conditions should demand higher pay, others might believe that high pay should be determined solely on the number of qualifications or the experience an individual brings to a job. To highlight these differences in opinion try the following exercise, first on your own and then as a group.

E XERCISE

Rank the jobs listed below in the order you think they should be paid. Call the one you think should be highest paid number 1, lowest paid number 17. You must justify your ranking at the end of the exercise. In your decision you could take into account the following:

* Skills/training/education
* Responsibility level
* Mental requirements
* Physical requirements
* Working conditions
* Danger/element of risk

Job	Rank order
Police officer	
Professional engineer	
Building site labourer	
Doctor	
Bus driver	
Teacher	
Ambulance officer	
Dentist	
Shop assistant	

Waiter/waitress
Cleaner
Fork-lift truck driver
Plumber
Barrister
Office clerk
Fire fighter
Word-processor operator

WAGE COUNCILS

In most industries and workplaces pay is set by voluntary agreements between employers and workers, but in some, wage councils set minimum rates of pay.

Wage councils are independent bodies appointed by the government. Each council is made up of representatives of employers and workers in the industry which it covers, together with three independent members. There are 26 councils. The main wage councils cover the retail trade, hotel and catering, hairdressing, clothing manufacture and laundries. The councils cover about 260,000 employers and some 2,500,000 workers. For workers aged 21 and over wage councils have the power to fix a:

- basic minimum hourly rate of pay;
- basic number of hours a week after which an overtime rate has to be paid;
- minimum hourly overtime rate of pay;
- limit on how much employers can deduct from wages for any living accomodation they provide.

DISCUSSION POINT

What are the benefits for employees in occupations covered by a wage council? Do you think all employers should be covered by wage council, or is it enough to rely on voluntary agreements between employers and trade unions?

If an employer fails to pay the wage council rate, he or she can be prosecuted by the Wages Inspectorate. Failure to pay the legal rate is a criminal offence. Employers covered by wage councils are also required to display the relevant notices and to keep adequate records of hours and wages.

THE PAYSLIP

Every person in a job must receive a payslip with their pay. This shows how take-home pay is worked out. There are two compulsory deductions on most peoples payslips: income tax and national insurance. These taxes go to the government to help pay for education, health services, social services, welfare benefits, pensions and defence. Income tax is a certain amount of money which is taken out of an employee's earnings every time he or she gets paid. The tax year is different to our ordinary calendar year, beginning on the 6 April one year and ending on the 5 April the next. The rate of contribution and earnings limit usually change every year. Each year, an employer has to give each employee a P60 form to show how much income tax has been paid. When an employee leaves a job, he or she should be given a P45 form to take to the next employer.

EXERCISE

People have different views about what makes a fair tax system. Some people might think that a good system is one which doesn't take too much money out of your earnings. Others might say that a good tax is one that raises a lot of revenue for the Chancellor of the Exchequer to distribute to local authorities to spend on hospitals, housing and education.

Make a list of what you think the following people might consider to be a good tax:

1 The Chancellor of the Exchequer
2 A hospital administrator or manager
3 A man or woman setting up a small business
4 An unemployed person

Why might different groups and individuals have different views about what is a fair tax system? Look up the latest income tax rates. What percentage of income would be paid by a single person with no extra allowances earning the following incomes:

- £5,000
- £10,000
- £15,000
- £20,000
- £50,000

While businesses which are not covered by wage councils are not obliged by law to pay a legal minimum rate, it is still good practice to pay employees the going rate for their skills. Some industries have nationally negotiated rates of pay for a whole range of employees, and even employers who are not members of the relevant employers' federation usually find it helpful to adopt these rates. Where nationally negotiated rates of pay are not available, it is possible to find out what the usual wages are by checking what other employers pay their employees for similar work.

GROSS PAY

Gross pay is the total amount of money received by an employee before any additional increments or deductions are made. For example, the gross pay may be set at £200 for a 37 hour week, but the amounts and reasons for any deductions must be shown on a pay statement.

NET PAY

Net pay is the amount of money an employee takes home after deductions. One of three conditions has to be met for an employer to make lawful deductions from wages or receive payment from an employee. These are that the deduction or payment:

- is required or authorised by the law (for example, income tax, national insurance or an order for an attachment of earnings by a court);
- is authorised by an employee's contract of employment, so long as a copy of the terms of the contract which authorises the deduction has been given to the employee before the deduction is made;
- was agreed by an employee in writing before it was made.

OTHER TYPES OF REWARD

OVERTIME PAY

Overtime is paid at a higher rate. The amount usually depends on how difficult it is to persuade the labour force to work extra or unsocial hours. While overtime worked during weekdays may need to be paid at, for example, one and a half times the basic hourly rate, on Saturdays and Sundays the rate may need to be increased to twice the hourly rate. Overtime is usually offered by firms where the amount of work varies considerably, and it is more economical to increase the hours for the existing workforce rather than take on more full-time staff

BONUS PAYMENTS

Bonus pay is used as an incentive to make employees work harder. Bonuses may be offered to encourage staff to meet certain targets, for example, to meet certain production deadlines or sales figures. It is common practice to offer a bonus at Christmas-time or just before the summer holidays or annual shutdown, when otherwise there may be a temptation to slacken off.

COMMISSION

Salespeople are very often rewarded according to the results they achieve. They may be allowed to take, for example, 10 per cent of the price of all sales they make.

Commission is used as an incentive for salespeople to increase the volume of their sales, and is usually paid in addition to the basic salary. Sometimes, however, commission pay is the only pay received for a job, so the incentive to work hard and achieve results is obviously increased.

DISCUSSION POINT

Look through your local newspaper at the job advertisements. Are there any jobs which are paid solely on the basis of sales made? What do you consider to be the advantages and disadvantages of commission-only jobs from the employer's and employee's points of view?

PIECE-RATE PAYMENTS

Piece-rate payments may be offered as an alternative to basic-time rates. Employees are rewarded according to the output they produce. When the work involved is of a precise nature and carefulness is extremely important, this is the least suitable method of payment, since it can cause employees to rush and make mistakes.

RETAINER FEE

This is a basic fee which is paid at regular intervals to maintain a worker's loyalty. Sometimes a retainer fee is given to keep a particular person under contract to a firm in the event of his or her skills being required. For example, a pool of firms in the same industry might 'retain' a management consultant to advise on a range of issues such as quality control, recruitment or health and safety regulations.

PERKS (NON-MONETARY REWARDS)

Many jobs include a wide range of fringe benefits which do not appear directly in the pay packet. Railway or airline employees and their families, for example, may benefit from free travel. Managerial jobs often include perks such as subsidised company cars and phone bills, private health costs and sometimes children's school fees. Other fringe benefits include:

- Subsidised canteen services
- Free training courses
- The right to buy the company products at discount prices

EXERCISE

Look through the situations vacant columns and job opportunities pages of local and national newspapers, or visit the job centre, careers office or a local recruitment agency. What fringe benefits, if any, are most commonly offered? Try to estimate these extras in terms of money; how much would the various perks amount to in the paypacket?

FACTORS WHICH INFLUENCE INCOME FROM EMPLOYMENT

A host of different factors will determine pay. Some of these are explained below.

QUALIFICATIONS AND SKILLS

Employees who have either developed their educational background or who have trained for a number of years to acquire a skill will expect to be rewarded for their expertise. For example, it takes many years of training and education to become a brain surgeon, and so surgeons expect a salary which rewards them for this hard work.

EXPERIENCE

Staff who have worked for an organisation for a long time are often paid at higher rates than new or recent recruits.

PAYMENT FOR RESULTS

Some employees' pay is directly linked to their output. In many industries workers are paid on piece-rates where their pay is directly linked to their measured output.

RESPONSIBILITY

People who undertake jobs involving supervision, decision taking and influencing the lives of others are often rewarded extra for this additional pressure. For example, it would be expected that a production manager earns more than a production line worker.

LOCATION

It is much more expensive for employees to live in the south-east of England than in other parts of the country such as the north-west. Many employers recognise this and provide allowances (such as the London allowance or weighting) to compensate for additional living costs.

DANGER OR RISK

Some jobs are dangerous and others are very unhealthy. Many employers take the nature of the work into consideration and try to provide a suitable pay scale. Examples of dangerous or risky jobs might include industrial cleaning, fire fighting and diving.

D ISCUSSION POINT

In some occupations employees may only work for a set number of hours, and work under very strict health and safety rules.

Working in twos, list 12 jobs which are either dangerous, unhealthy or dirty. Discuss your findings with other members of the group. What solutions can you think of which might reduce the risk?

SUPPLY AND DEMAND OF LABOUR

If labour is in short supply and the demand for a particular skill is high, employers will often be prepared to pay higher rates to engage suitable staff.

APPLICATION OF THESE FACTORS

We can apply these pay determining factors in a number of examples:

1 A doctor earns more than a hospital porter or auxillary nurse because of his or her:
   (a) qualifications
   (b) extensive overtime
   (c) skill and responsibility
   (d) decision making which affects other peoples lives

2 A 55-year-old worker may earn more than an 18-year-old who does the same job because of his or her:
   (a) skills and experience
   (b) loyalty
   (c) annual pay increments

3 A bank clerk in London may earn more than a bank clerk in Newcastle because of:
   (a) the need to compensate for the expense of living in the south-east
   (b) a greater demand for bank clerks in the south-east, together with a shortage of qualified labour in that area

HOLIDAYS

It is customary for employers to give employees a paid holiday each year. The UK is one of the few countries in the European Community where virtually no worker has a statutory right to holiday leave and pay. However, a survey in 1990 (published in the journal *Bargaining Report*) estimated that over 80 per cent of British workers now have 21 or more days paid holiday a year as well as public holidays. For most workers, holiday entitlements are governed by their contract of employment rather than national laws. The amount of holiday leave set for employees will obviously depend on a number of factors such as the industry they work in and their length of service. For example, in the public sector's careers service an employee with under five years service receives 20 days holiday plus bank holidays, and an employee with over five years service receives 25 days plus bank holidays.

There are a number of industry-wide agreements which have set recommended annual leave levels. In general, it is assumed that there is a reasonable period of leave. Many firms have set between four and five weeks a year as a reasonable amount. Any changes to the annual leave entitlements must be negotiated and agreed between employers and employees or between managers and trade unions. It is good practice to include holiday entitlement details in an employee's written statement of terms or employment contract, with details of when the holiday year begins and ends. For example, from 1st April one year to 31st March the next. The contract or written statement should also contain details of entitlements to public holidays.

EXERCISE

In pairs, interview a range of employees from different industries. Ask them:

*   how many days annual leave are they allowed;
*   whether the holidays are set, for example, by factory shutdowns, or whether they are free to take them when they like.

Discuss your findings among your group.

FURTHER READING

Armstrong, M. & H. Murlis, *Reward management: a handbook of salary administration* Kogan Page, 1991

Hewitt Associates, *Total compensation management: reward management strategies for the 1990s* Blackwell, 1992

12

EXTERNAL INFLUENCES ON THE UK LABOUR MARKET

Just as no company can exist without customers, suppliers, buyers and clients, a country also relies on other countries for its economic survival. The world consists of importers and exporters; while a country might specialise in exporting gold for example, it also imports a steady flow of other goods.

What a country produces is heavily influenced by its geography and climate. Warm countries tend to export quite a lot of food products, especially non-meat products such as fruit, vegetables, tea and coffee which will not grow in cooler climates. Countries which are landlocked and have no fishing industry are likely to import more fish than those countries surrounded by sea such as the United Kingdom. A country's imports are also influenced by its economic position: a poor country is far less likely to import hundreds of expensive cars than a rich country might. During an economic peak a higher number of luxury goods tend to be imported than in a recession.

EXERCISE

Ten countries and ten export products are listed at random below. Try to match the product with its country of origin.

New Zealand	Copper and zinc
Morocco	wood
Kenya	pharmaceutical goods and watches
Thailand	animals and animal products
Finland	wine
Switzerland	tea
India	wool
Argentina	tapioca products and rice
France	fish
Zambia	coffee

Look through an encyclopaedia to check how accurate you were.

Exporting goods relies heavily on a country's transport system. Small goods such as pencils or pens can easily be exported between countries by aircraft or in small quantities simply by post. Large products, however, such as ships or cars, rely on a well-organised shipping industry to export and import them.

EXERCISE

Taking two of the products listed above in the exports exercise, name the jobs which would be involved in the entire process from manufacture to delivering them to their final destination. If we assume that the transport method is the 'go between', what other jobs do you think would come before and after the product is transported? A woollen jumper, for example, would include shepherds, sheep farmers, sheep shearers, dyers, customs officials, buyers and suppliers, fashion designers and shop assistants. Present the jobs involved in the manufacture and delivery of your two chosen products as flowcharts to the rest of the group.

THE SINGLE EUROPEAN MARKET

On 31 December 1992, the twelve member states of the European Community joined forces to become the single European market.

The twelve member countries (in alphabetical order) are:
Belguim, France, Denmark, Germany, Greece, Ireland, Italy, Luxemburg, The Netherlands, Portugal, Spain and the United Kingdom.

The whole process of becoming a single market started much earlier than 1992. It began in 1957 when the six founder member countries formed the European Economic Community (EEC). They were Belgium, France, Italy, Luxemburg, The Netherlands and West Germany. The UK became committed in 1973 when it too became a member. The concept of a truly common market was strengthened in 1985 by the introduction of a new law: the Single Market Act. This Act came into force on 1 July 1987.

MAIN AIMS AND OBJECTIVES

The single European market will gradually increase competition for jobs, for prices, for products and for workers. Many people think that the single market is a non-event. They are partly right, the single market in which most trade barriers between EC countries will disappear is not an event. It is a process which will affect all of us for the rest of our lives. The European Community, founded over 30 years ago is now a unique group of 12 countries. The main objective of the EC is to enable goods, services and people to move as easily between countries as they can within countries.

Included in the EC's programme of 300 proposals are plans to:

- remove legal barriers restricting the free movement of goods, services and people throughout the Community;
- reduce taxes on diesel and petrol fuels;
- ensure freedom for people to work where they like;
- recognise qualifications throughout the Community to eliminate the need for certain professions to requalify if they move to another member country;
- standardise the retirement age for men and women. At present, in most member countries women retire a few years earlier than men;

- standardise maternity rights for women within the Community;
- standardise VAT rates;
- stabilise currency exchange rates, with the possible creation of a single European currency.

Above all, the EC is a giant step towards a closer alliance among the people of Europe.

EXERCISE

Select a couple of national daily newspapers. Cut out the articles with the words EC or Europe in their title. How much of the news is dedicated to events on a European scale, rather than merely national news? Visit a large public library which keeps back-copies of newspapers. Compare the amount of European news in today's newspapers with that in the same newspapers a decade, or even five years, ago. Very likely, you will notice a far higher profile is given to Europe today.

As far as the 1990s are concerned the single European market will certainly go down in European history books, probably more so than any other single event of the late twentieth century. The changes will affect all aspects of life, from the obvious economic and political changes to the less obvious cultural and social changes. The changes which the single market brings will demand a range of new or improved skills in order to take advantage of new European opportunities. In order to achieve this an enormous number of changes will have to be made in key areas of business including:

- Company law
- Product development and manufacture
- Production standards
- Professional qualifications
- Language training
- Recruitment policies
- Information systems
- Transport and distribution

EXERCISE

Taking just one of the changes mentioned above, how might a company plan in order to cope with it successfully? Find out about local and national sources of information and assistance which a company might use. For example, chambers of commerce have European sections, many cities have European Information Centres (EICs). The Department of Trade and Industry (DTI) has a single market telephone hotline. What other sources of information are available in your area?

The majority of single market measures are already in force; in fact, over 80 per cent of the measures needed to accomplish a single market have already been agreed by the Council of Ministers, the most powerful decision making body within the European Community structure.

NEW STRATEGIES FOR MARKETING

The pace of change for businesses has grown in recent years to the point where the only certainty seems to be one of continuing change. In light of the single market, many enterprising businesses have already forged partnerships with other organisations in Europe. A business partnership, well researched and organised, is an exciting and profitable way to run a business. Within the single market, no one partner is more important than the other: everyone must be on equal terms. Equal opportunities for all EC citizens is essential, and the formal measures which the EC equality programmes have established should ensure this happens.

It is important to remember that the single market is a third larger than the American market and more than double the Japanese market; it would be impossible therefore for even the most successful company to sell single-handedly to the entire European business community. In order to ensure that products, services, price and quality meet customer needs, key questions will need to be addressed including:

- What new customers can we reach?
- Should priority be focused on the wider market or should it be concentrated on trading locally?
- How does one acquire the right market information and can one afford to ignore the cultural and economic differences between member countries?
- What new competition can be expected?
- Are we organised within the business to learn about the single market and to promote our products and services effectively?

At first, a product may not seem to have any outlets if just a survey of the national market is carried out, whereas a European market survey could possibly show that some countries are very interested in it. Also, if a European angle is included from the outset when a product is launched, a firm achieves a quicker return on investment. For smaller firms, experience tends to show that the best way for a smaller firm to reach the European market is to link up with partners in the same sector in a chosen country. For example, a toothbrush manufacturer in the UK, based in Merseyside, might be better off concentrating, not on the entire 12, not even on a single country such as Spain, but on an area within his or her selected country, which is as easily manageable as the home market. In the case of Spain, for instance, Andalusia or Catalonia may be appropriate targets, more likely to produce results than a campaign aimed at the whole country.

Sources of help with marketing are:

- Chambers of commerce
- Training and Enterprise Councils (TECs)
- Market Research Society
- Foreign trade directories
- Banks
- Trade associations

Contact one or two large companies in your area. Are they involved in exporting their products to another country within the single market? If so, how did they find their customers in the first place, and what kind of marketing strategy did they use ? Present your findings in report form to your group.

BETTER TRAINING REQUIRED

A well-trained workforce is the key factor which will determine the success or failure of any large scale project such as the single market. There can be little prospect of success unless the workforce is equipped with first class and up-to-date knowledge within its particular field or specialism. This means that an organisation must provide a whole range of facilities such as training programmes, conferences, guest speakers, visits, exchanges and language training.

Apart from inviting guest speakers, running training courses and circulating specialist magazines, how else might an organisation ensure that its workforce is kept up to date in its particular field?

Apart from traditional approaches to training such as apprenticeships and trainee-ships, many companies are now introducing a range of special measures with external support from these two sources:

- the UK TEC network, for information on courses, grants, overseas exchanges, recruitment planning, and much more;
- the EC research programmes and exchange programmes, such as PETRA, ERASMUS, COMETT, LINGUA and TEMPUS, to mention just a few.

Try and find out if any organisation in your area is involved in any of the EC programmes listed above. You might be able to find this information from a European Information Centre if there is one in your area, the chamber of commerce or local TEC. Research one of the programmes and present a summary of its contents to your group.

Adapting to the single market may well mean training existing staff in new skills. Training is likely to be an increasingly important means of survival in a very competitive and rapidly changing environment. Training programmes ought to be built into each organisation's business plan. Very often, staff already possess the necessary know-how and practical job experience. It is up to human resource and personnel departments to make full use of the potential in their workforces.

For help with training, recruitment and languages the following sources may be useful:

- TECs

- Industrial Training Organisations (ITOs)
- Language Export Centres
- Institute of Linguists
- Training Access Points (TAPs)

EXERCISE

Try to find out what is available for companies in your area by way of assistance in planning and delivering business skills training, and foreign language courses. A good place to start is the local TEC. Also, scan the local newspapers for information on courses in the area.

WORLD ECONOMIC DEVELOPMENTS

The move towards a single European market has also exerted a powerful hold on European countries which are not members of the European Community. While many European countries are not in the single market, can it really be called such?

Scandinavian and East European countries are among the main omissions, and the impact they are likely to have on the single market remains to be seen. It will take at least five years of established single market experience to provide an accurate picture of the influence of non-EC members on the single market. Many single market regulations apply equally to the whole of Europe and all of them have an impact on employment. Proposals and events which might influence the Europe of the future include:

- joint financial and economic initiatives: if a European Central Bank were to become a reality, this would imply the need for changes for individual countries;
- social welfare will most likely change: current differences in levels of provision between each country are sure to make the less well off put pressure on their governments for change;
- environmental issues and green politics will also affect the whole of Europe;
- defence issues: will they be jointly decided at Brussels or will each member country make their own arrangements?
- population changes in the European labour market, influenced by the decline in the birthrate and increased life expectancy, are set to influence employers recruitment and selection patterns;
- world economic developments, particularly the influence of Japan, the United States and the Third World.

JAPAN

Japan has a population of over 120 million. Its main exports are chemicals, electronic goods, machinery and transport, optical equipment, ships and textiles. In the 1960s and 1970s Japan became one of the world's great industrial powers. Japan is a world leader in the production of motor cycles, merchant ships and television sets. Only the USA produces more motor vehicles and Hong Kong more radios. It has a wide range of light and heavy industry and is the world's third largest producer of electrical energy after the US and CIS. Japan's main industrial regions are in the coastal lowlands between Tokyo and northern Kyushu.

Japanese working habits are different from those in the UK and the rest of Europe. Stress at work has become a major cause of illness. In fact, stress is a problem which has reached epidemic proportions in Japan. They have a word for it, *karoshi*: sudden death from stress or overwork. Every year almost 10,000 Japanese literally work themselves into the grave.

The Japanese work much harder, officially 400 hours a year harder, than their European counterparts. Unofficially they work even longer than that, and many do not work set hours or get paid for overtime. The biggest car workers union in the country wants working hours reduced to 1,800 a year. Few Japanese workers take more than seven day's holiday a year. There appears to be three main reasons for this:

* intense competition between individuals and between companies;
* loyalty to the company;
* a belief that their standard of living depends on long hours and hard work.

Commuting long distances increases stress for the Japanese worker. A *karoshi* 'hotline' was set up in late 1991 and more that 60 per cent of the women who rang complained that their husbands or sons rarely returned home before 11 p.m. The situation is getting worse as the Japanese population declines. Nowadays there are 140 vacancies to every 11 job seekers. By the year 2000 the net shortages of workers will increase to 2.6 million. The problem is made worse by Japanese attitudes and prejudice against women and immigrants. In the late twentieth century women are still expected to give up paid employment outside the home as soon as they get married.

So what does this mean for the rest of the world? Many Americans believe that overwork and underpay give Japanese companies an unfair competitive edge. The International Educational Development Inc, a US-based organisation, goes so far as to accuse Japan of violating the Universal Declaration of Human Rights by refusing workers 'rest and leisure, including reasonable limitation of working hours and periodic holidays with pay'.

It would be impossible not to have noticed the steady growth of manufactured goods from Japan in the European market during the past two decades. More recently, the arrival in Britain of a number of major Japanese manufacturers such as Nissan, Toshiba, Isuzu and Hitachi has generated a lot of interest in Japanese employment practices. These companies have brought with them a number of changes which have influenced traditional British industry. These include:

* the single-union 'no strike' deals at firms like Toshiba, Hitachi and Nissan;
* abolishing status divisions and inequality between management and workers, such as separate canteens, car parks and different types of working uniform;
* the introduction of quality circles and other group-based methods of involving workers in the quality of production;

- high levels of employee commitment to the finished product and to the quality of work produced.

EXERCISE

Find out if there are any Japanese companies in your area. If possible, arrange to visit them and try to find out what their attitudes are towards various business activities, such as the role of management and employees, hours of work, perks and benefits, holidays and pensions, quality circles and worker participation. How do they differ from a British company?

THE UNITED STATES OF AMERICA

The USA is a federal republic and the world's fourth largest nation. The bulk of the USA lies between Canada in the North and Mexico in the South. The 49th state, Alaska, is in north-western North America while the 50th state, Hawaii, is in the north Pacific Ocean. The capital is Washington DC, and other large cities include New York City, Chicago, Los Angeles, Houston and Detroit.

Large scale industrialisation caused the economy to expand in the late nineteenth century. Between the two World Wars there was a severe economic depression, but after World War II the USA accepted its role as a superpower. Its advanced technology was highlighted by its feat of landing men on the moon in 1969.

The United States is the world's most industrialised nation, accounting for about half of all the world's industrial goods. It is one of the world's top producers of copper, iron ore, oil and natural gas, lead, phosphates, sulphur and uranium. Its main exports are machinery, vehicles, grains, aircraft, chemicals, coal, textiles, cotton, iron and steel goods.

In recent history the USA and Europe have enjoyed good economic and political relations. As from 1992, the 12 member countries are in effect a United Europe, possibly to be seen by the rest of the world as the United States has been.

THE THIRD WORLD

Many poorer countries are also the world's warmest countries and it is estimated that they grow most of the world's food. However, they receive very little reward for doing so and therefore remain caught in a poverty trap. How does the Third World fit into the single European market? Many organisations already import a large amount of raw materials from Third World countries. Other organisations work closely with Third World countries, towards developing educational and industrial enterprises. Some companies do this from a charity perspective, while others build relationships for profit.

DISCUSSION POINT

What are the main reasons why a UK company might import its raw materials from a Third World country? How can a Third World economy improve if developed countries exploit them for the cheapness of their labour and raw materials?

New EC immigration policies may have an adverse effect on future relationships with Third World countries. In many instances pools of workers are drawn in from poorer countries when the demand for labour is high, and sent back when the demand is reduced. In general these temporary workers have little or none of the legal rights which full citizens have.

DISCUSSION POINT

It is generally accepted that the single European market will eventually bring an increase in employment opportunities, and create a wealthier Europe. What effects may these developments have on Third World countries?

FURTHER READING

Oliver, N. & B. Wilkinson, *The Japanization of British industry* Blackwell, 1988
Teague, P. *The European Community: the social dimension* Kogan Page, 1989

recommendations
to have
HRM
+ performance

13

RECOMMENDATIONS FOR EFFECTIVE HUMAN RESOURCE MANAGEMENT

SUMMARY

The wide range of working methods and conditions in the 1990s and beyond mean that no two workplaces are identical. What might be a suitable policy for one business to adopt might be totally unsuitable for another. Policy and practice which govern working relations and regulations, influence organisations. Organisations also, in turn, influence policy and practice. Whatever the size or nature of an organisation, effective use of human resources is the main component of business success. The competitiveness of the late twentieth century global economy means that people cannot be overlooked, as they represent the main resource available to companies. We could use the following formula to embody the four most important elements of good human resource management:

Four P formula = People, Policies, Planning and Participation

To put the 4P formula into a meaningful framework for action, the term human resource can be used as an acronym, on which to hang the key words for an effective personnel and recruitment strategy:

H: HUMAN BEINGS

Employees are more likely to behave well under conditions in which they are treated well. On the other hand they are likely to behave badly when they are treated badly. So a well-planned programme of staff development coupled with a high regard for staff welfare should act as the key element within any organisation. The spin-offs to be gained from a happy and well-trained workforce are likely to include:

- an increase in motivation and morale;
- an increase in productivity;
- a better company image;
- high staff retention rate which avoids the need of constant recruitment.

U: USEFULNESS

Every member of an organisation should be given useful employment in order to reach their full potential. This benefits both employers and employees alike.

M: MOTIVATION

A good human resource programme will have staff motivation high up on its agenda. A well-motivated workforce helps to eliminate problems associated with boredom, lethargy, disruptiveness and bad attendance.

D ISCUSSION POINT

What steps can an organisation take to increase
Working in twos, make a list called, 'motivators
When each pair's contribution has been preser
group on a flipchart: how many motivators hav

Motivation
A well managed
human

A: APPRAISAL

If management interest goes no further than
nothing to prevent an employee progressively
does not care for, to concentrate on those he
often happens in organisations which fail to
performance. A good system of open staff aj
and reached in the coming year are jointly
plan of action.

N: NEGOTIATION

It is far better to negotiate working arrai
employment, rather than impose them. Encouraging staff to inject them
enables them to believe in the rules and regulations, which is more likely to produce a better working climate than one where rules are imposed and perhaps staff see little point in them.

R: RECRUITMENT

If recruitment and selection are right and attract the people who will do the job right, they will bring the right performance. Having the right people with the right skills in the right job justifies any expense of a good recruitment policy. When an organisation gets the wrong people, it is very expensive.

E: EMPLOYEE RELATIONS

A good employee relations policy should aim to ensure that it is:

- simple and straightforward;
- controllable;
- open to change and improvements, not rigid.

S: STAFF PARTICIPATION

Staff should be allowed and encouraged to contribute their own ideas and suggestions, and the traditional organisational norms should not be the only working methods which count.

O: OPINIONS

Value the opinions of everyone involved in the workforce and encourage staff to participate. The earlier such participation is encouraged, the more effective all employment practices will be.

U: USEFULNESS

Investment in training increases the usefulness of the human resources available to an organisation. This investment should be regarded as part of an organisation's strategy to achieve overall company success.

R: REWARDS

These should be provided as incentives, and as a means of ensuring that key staff are acknowledged.

C: COMMUNICATION

Communication can be either formal (memoranda, notices, reports, summaries) or informal, such as through the grapevine. The best communication relies on both methods as a means of exchanging information and keeping staff well informed.

E: EFFECTIVE PEOPLE MANAGEMENT

Good employers do not happen by accident. The companies in which people thrive have well-thought out human resource programmes and management policies.

LONG-TERM SUCCESS

To achieve long-term success, the following 10 requirements must be stated and followed:

1 That the principle of open, honest internal communication be supported by the top executive with the assurance that such communication is an essential part of effective management.
2 That employees be informed of and encouraged to share in company goals, objectives and plans. In large organisations, this should be done in company publications, at departmental meetings, and through staff appraisals.
3 That employees be informed and kept up to date about all on-going company activities. Remember: nothing annoys employees more than learning from an outsider about some activity, problem or event in which his or her organisation is involved.
4 That employees be informed of contentious, delicate and negative issues. These issues might include recruitment problems, a drop in production or sales, staffing cutbacks, a decline in profits, termination of contracts, etc.
5 That all managers actively support the human resource management policies, in practice as well as in theory. They must also realise that it is not a matter of personal choice; it is an obligation they must adhere to daily.
6 That management learn to listen and to encourage a continual flow of upward communication concerning staff's ideas, suggestions and problems.
7 That management recognise and act upon the average employee's desire to assist his or her company to achieve company goals.
8 That top executives and boards of directors recognise that human resource management must be planned and organised, and that communication and participation are vital ingredients of company success. It is important to have one person in charge of internal and external communication policy and practice. That person can ensure that communication policies are followed in a

consistent method in all parts of the organisation, in all company publications, and in all employment activities.

9 That management and all other personnel who are responsible for staff examine career development and staff welfare issues regularly. They should discuss with staff ways in which such developments may be improved and, if appropriate, consider what training might be required. In order to assist this, management should liaise with useful local organisations such as local colleges, training providers and TECs.

10 That management provide financial support for all employment policies. The allocation of adequate funding is essential for transforming policy into practice.

Organisations which meet these requirements and respond to the needs of their employees stand a higher chance of success in the increasingly competitive world economic market than those which ignore them. Organisations which are committed to effective human resource management feel a responsibility towards their personnel, and work to ensure that their employees' skills and wellbeing are continuously maintained and improved. Evidence shows that, in the majority of organisations, a dynamic human resource policy is the most efficient means of motivating staff, encouraging high staff retention rates and low rates of absenteeism, and increasing morale, all the factors which, together, will dramatically increase an organisations' chance of success.

FURTHER READING

Attwood, M. *Personnel Management* Macmillan, 1992

Johnson, R. *How to manage people* Hutchinson, 1984

Little, R. *Communication at work* Pitman, 1987

Sisson, K. (ed.) *Personnel management in Britain* Blackwell, 1989

Smithson, S. & J. Whitehead, *Business communication* Croner Publication, 1987

Young, A. (ed.) *The manager's handbook: the practical guide to successful management* Sphere, 1986

APPENDICES

APPENDIX 1: GLOSSARY OF TERMS

Arbitration   The process of resolving disputes by bringing in a third party.

Arbitrator   Person appointed by the government to help settle disputes.

Capital   Money invested in a business by its owners in order to earn income.

Closed shop   An agreement between an employer and a trade union that all employees should belong to the same union.

Code of practice   Documents issued by the government or a governing body such as the Commission for Racial Equality to provide guidance on a specific topic. A code of practice can be quoted in legal cases.

Collective agreement   An agreement reached between management and trade unions which covers a particular working group.

Collective bargaining   The process through which management representatives and union representatives jointly make collective agreements. Collective bargaining is applied to those negotiations specifically concerned with the changing of terms and conditions of employment, for example, a change in the normal working hours.

Conciliation   The process of resolving disputes by involving a third party who does not make a decision but tries to aid the process of reaching agreements.

Contract of employment   The legal relationship between employers and employees, governing what an employee must do and what he or she must receive in conditions and wages.

Corporate culture   Unwritten set of values and rules within an organisation conditioning the behaviour of those belonging to it.

Corporate strategy   Assessment of the relationship between an organisation and its environment resulting in a plan to achieve its business objectives.

Disciplinary procedure   The methods, often agreed between management and trade unions or employees for dealing with shortcomings in employees conduct and behaviour.

Discrimination   Occurs when one person or group of people is treated less fairly than another group, usually on the grounds of sex or race.

Dismissal   The ending of an employee's employment with an organisation. The procedure for dismissing an employee must be fair, for example, several warnings must be given to an employee before he or she is dismissed.

Dispute   An unresolved issue between employees and their employer. A disputes procedure is the method agreed by employers and employees which they will follow in order to resolve the dispute.

Elected representatives   Those people who through a method of voting have been given authority to act on behalf of a group of employees. Often referred to as shop stewards.

Employee relations   A general term to describe the way that people at work behave and relate to each other and to the organisation as a whole.

Employers' association   An organisation of employers in the same industry. Sometimes an association will negotiate on behalf of the employers with the trade unions representing the employees of the member organisation and establish national agreements. Sometimes referred to as employers' federations.

European Community   The idea of the European Community came as people wanted to develop a peaceful and prosperous Europe after 1945. At present there are 12 nations in the EC: France, UK, Italy, Germany, The Netherlands, Ireland, Belgium, Spain, Greece, Luxembourg, Portugal and Denmark. There are four main institutions involved in running the European Community. These are;

1 The Council of Ministers
2 The European Commission
3 The European Parliament
4 The Court of Justice

Flexitime or FWT   Arrangements where individual employees can choose the time at which they start and finish work between certain core hours. Normally there has to be a minimum of hours worked within a given period, usually four weeks.

Genuine Occupational Qualification (GOQ)   Reasons such as authenticity or decency which are allowed by law to exempt the employer from the Sex Discrimination Act and the Race Relations Act.

Grievance   A complaint or problem raised formally by an employee.

Grievance procedure   A formal process, often agreed between management and employees or their union for resolving grievances.

Gross misconduct   Certain actions in breach of a company's rules which are generally considered to be so unreasonable that they lead to instant dismissal.

Guarantee payments   Statutory payments which an employer must make to workers laid off or on short time.

Health and Safety representative   A person elected to help monitor health and safety practices and employee welfare.

Induction training   Training to introduce new employees to their place of work and to their job.

Job sharing   This means two people agreeing to share one full-time job.

Lay off   Temporary suspension of the contract of employment usually because no work is available.

National Insurance   National Insurance is paid by most working people over 16 years of age. The money is used, among other things, by the government to pay for social security benefits and pensions.

National official   A full-time official employed by a union, usually based at its head office. National officials usually have trade or industry responsibilities, or a given geographical area to cover.

Negotiation   The process whereby elected or nominated representatives for different groups discuss an issue in order to achieve a satisfactory solution for the parties concerned.

Participation   Refers to the wide variety of methods and activities through which employees are involved in the decision making processes of their organisation.

Personnel department   A specialist department in large organisations concerned with the people employed in the organisation, and the policies and practices which regulate employment.

Probationary period   A fixed time which will vary between organisations during which a new employee will have to achieve a satisfactory work standard and only after which permanent employment will commence.

Procedures   Set methods for dealing with workplace issues usually connected with grievances and disciplines.

Redundancy   Occurs when a worker or workers are no longer required by an organisation, because either their continued employment or their skills are surplus to requirements.

Shop floor   A workplace or department usually implying a production department.

Strike   The stoppage of work by employees as a collective breach of their contracts of employment, but with the intention of returning to work at a later date.

Terms and conditions   What is expected of an employee and what an employee can expect from working for an organisation, for instance, basic payment rates, holidays, overtime pay.

Trade union   An association of people in employment who have joined together to maintain or improve their working conditions. Trade unions work for a fair deal for all workers.

Welfare benefits   There are three types of welfare benefits:

Non-contributory benefits which an individual can claim because he or she is part of a group of people entitled to claim them, for example, someone who is bringing up a child on his or her own can claim child benefit.

Contributory benefits Only if enough National Insurance contributions have been paid can someone claim one of these benefits, for example, unemployment benefit.

Means-tested benefits These are special need payments. Whether a person is entitled to them depends on his or her income, outgoings and savings, in other words their 'means'. They also include income support and housing benefit.

Written statement   For most employees an employer is obliged by law to provide a written statement (under the Employment Protection (consolidation) Act 1978) containing at least the main points of the contract of employment, within the first 13 weeks of the employee starting work.

APPENDIX 2: LAWS

ACTS OF PARLIAMENT

1944 The Disabled Persons (Employment) Act
1958 The Disabled Persons (Employment) Act
1969 Employers' Liability (Compulsory Insurance) Act
1970 Equal Pay Act
1974 The Health and Safety at Work Act
1975 Sex Discrimination Act
1976 Race Relations Act
1978 Employment Protection (Consolidation) Act
1981 Disabled Persons Act
1984 Data Protection Act
1984 Trade Union Act
1986 Education Act
1986 Wages Act
1988 Local Government Act
1989 Employment Act
1992 Further and Higher Education Act
1992 Education (Schools) Act
1992 Charities Act

EUROPEAN COMMUNITY LAW

Outlined below are summaries of the different types of European Community measures in use.

DIRECTIVES
A Directive is a European Community law which is legally binding on all member states. In most cases this means that national legislation has to be proposed or current laws have to be changed in order that they comply with the Directive's requirements.

REGULATIONS
A regulation is a law which is binding in all member states but does not require any national legislation to be implemented.

DECISIONS
Decisions can be issued either by the Council of Ministers or by the European Commission. They are legally binding on those to whom they are addressed. They may be addressed either to a member state, a company or to an individual.

RECOMMENDATIONS AND OPINIONS
Neither recommendations nor opinions have any legally binding effect. They are not laws. Instead, they state the view of the institution that issues them (in general, the European Commission), and they may encourage or suggest that certain action be taken.

APPENDIX 3: ADDRESS LIST

Advisory, Conciliation and Arbitration Service Regional Offices (ACAS)

Northern Region
Westgate House
Westgate Road
Newcastle upon Tyne
NE1 1TJ

Yorkshire and Humberside Region
Commerce House
St Alban's Place
Leeds
LS2 8HH

South East Region
Westminster House
125 Fleet Road
Fleet
Aldershot
Hampshire
GU13 8PD

South West Region
Regent House
27a Regent Street
Clifton
Bristol
BS8 4HR

London Region
Clifton House
83 Euston Road
London
NW1 2RB

Midlands Region
Leonard House
319–323 Bradford Street
Birmingham
B5 6ET

Nottingham Office
Anderson House
Clinton Avenue
Nottingham
NG5 1AW

North West Region
Boulton House
17 Chorlton Street
Manchester
M1 3HY

Merseyside Office
Cressington House
249 St Mary's Road
Garston
Liverpool
L19 ONF

Scotland
Franborough House
123 Bothwell Street
Glasgow
G2 7JR

Wales
Phase 1
Ty Glas Road
Llanishen
Cardiff
CF4 5PH

Age Concern (England)
Astral House
1268 London Road
London
SW16 4ER

Apex Trust
2–4 Colchester Street
London
E1 7PG

British Council of Organisations of Disabled People (BCODP)
St Mary's Church
Greenland Street
Woolwich
London
SE18 5AR

Business In The Community (BITC)
Opportunity 2000
Campaign Director
5 Cleveland Place
London
SW1Y 6JJ

Business & Technology Education Council (BTEC)
Central House
Upper Woburn Place
London
WC1H OHH

Commission for Racial Equality (CRE)
Elliot House
10–12 Allington Street
London
SW1 5EH

Commission of the European Communities
Jean Monnet House
8 Storey's Gate
London
SW1 P3AT

**Confederation of
British Industry
(CBI)**
Centre Point
103 New Oxford Street
London
WC1A 1DU

**Data Protection
Registrar**
Springfield House
Water Lane
Wilmslow
Cheshire
SK9 5AX

**Department of
Education and
Science (DES)**
Elizabeth House
York Road
London
SE1 7PH

**Department of
Employment**
Caxton House
Tothill Street
London
SW1H 9NF

**Department of Trade
& Industry (DTI)**
Telephone hotline: 081
200 1992

**Employers Forum on
Disability**
5 Cleveland Place
London
SW1Y 6JJ

**Equal Opportunities
Commission**
Overseas House
Quay Street
Manchester
M3 3HN

**Health and Safety
Executive
Information Centres**

Broad Lane
Sheffield
S3 7HQ

Baynards House
1 Chepstow Place
Westbourne Grove
London
W2 4TF

**Institute of Personnel
Management**
IPM House
Camp House
Wimbledon
London
SW19 4UX

National AIDS Trust
14th Floor, Euston
Tower
286 Euston Road
London
NW1 3DN

**National Council for
Vocational
Qualifications
(NCVQ)**
222 Euston Road
London
NW1 2BZ

**The Pathway
Employment Service**
169a City Road
Cardiff
CF2 3JB

**The Pre-Retirement
Association (PRA)**
19 Undine Street
London
SW17 8PP

**Royal Association for
Disability and
Rehabilitation
(RADAR)**
25 Mortimer Street
London
W1N 8AB

**Scottish Vocational
Education Council
(SCOTVEC)**
Hanover House
24 Douglas Street
Glasgow
G2 7NQ

**Training, Enterprise
and Education
Directorate (TEED)**
Department of
Employment
Moorfoot
Sheffield
S1 4PQ
(For information on
your local TEC)

**Trades Union Congress
(TUC)**
Congress House
23–28 Gt Russell Street
London
WC1B 3LS